VERNON AREA PUBLIC LIBRARY

012

Write Away!

LITERARY MAGAZINE

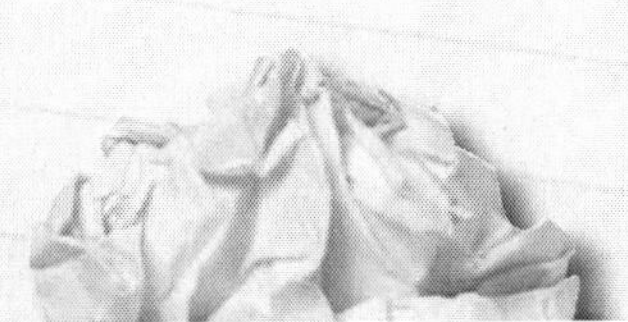

Published in Lincolnshire, Illinois

ISBN 978-0-9856586-0-1

Dear Reader,

We are extremely pleased to present the first annual *Write Away! Literary Magazine* featuring the creative writing of our young patrons in grades 3–8. Congratulations to all of our authors who are now published!

The Literary Magazine grew out of the Write Away! creative writing program. Once a month in the fall and spring, the library offers this writing workshop for kids to have fun exercising their imaginations on paper. Some of the stories in this year's magazine were based on prompts from Write Away! sessions. All the writing pieces are shining examples of the power of creative thought and the written word.

We hope you enjoy reading the work of these talented young authors!

Vernon Area Public Library
Youth Services

Table of Contents

LOST with Crocks

Abby K.

The Australian swamp, covered with scattered leaves and trees with vines dangling was peaceful and way warmer then snowy, freezing Illinois. Birds chirped and there were ripples in the swamp water as we passed.

Our tour guide whispered and answered questions as we walked along the pebble path. My brother and I fell behind goofing off and annoying each other, as usual.

In one moment, our tour group crossed paths with a much faster paced tour group. Andrew and I followed the wrong and much faster paced tour group by accident. Of course, my brother and I, not paying attention, just kept annoying each other and walked along like nothing happened.

A leaf crunched under my shoe and startled me so I glanced up. My glance turned into a stare. Then... I realized we were LOST in the Australian swamp. A bad thing since there are many predators out there hidden in the landscape and poised to attack!

I knew immediately if we didn't find our way out ASAP, we would be a snack in a flash. My brother and I heard a rustle in the leaves, we saw green scales glinting in the sun complete with bared yellow teeth full of blood from some unlucky victim.

The sun started to set and I thought we were going to be dinner very quickly if we didn't find our hotel resort. Trying not to turn my back on the crocodiles, I glanced upward finding myself gazing right into the bark of a tree branch.

"Andrew", I whispered, "Do you think we could climb the tree to safety?"

He looked at me with a pale face and nodded, his face full of hope.

The crocks were about 8 feet long and a murky shade of green. Two more had crawled out of the water. "This will only work if we jump at the same time and if we climb up the tree fast," I whispered even quieter than before. The crocodiles had moved in about a foot closer. I wished we had paid attention to my mom and dad and stayed with the tour group.

I nodded my head at my brother to signal him to jump at that moment with all of his might. I pushed upward and grabbed onto the branch, like a sloth, but my fingers were sweaty and I slipped... inch by inch my fingers slipped off.

But I had a plan, the soles of my shoes had gotten a grip on the bark as my brother was making his way to the top of the tree. I pushed up with my feet.

Luckily my friend, Jessica, had taught me how to climb trees and I found I passed my brother who was very slow at climbing trees.

As we neared the top, we saw a rescue helicopter in the distance and raced our way to the top of the canopy, grabbing random branches as fast as monkeys. When we reached the top, in the distance we saw the whirring of a helicopter. My brother and I signaled the helicopter by throwing leaves in the air. As it flew toward us, I noticed my mom and dad inside, with worried faces and tears everywhere.

The rescue people in neon suits threw down a safety rope. I grabbed on first and and Andrew grabbed after me. We started climbing as fast as we could climb. I looked down and my brother's face was so white. He looked as if he couldn't hold on any longer. Andrew's eyes were bulging and his mouth was open with a silent scream. I think he thought I was about to fall onto him and bring us both down into trouble again.

I was determined not to let go. I could hold on like that for hours; I was so comfortable. My calmness encouraged my brother to keep climbing and not give up. I grabbed onto the helicopter with slippery hands but luckily my dad caught my shirt before I fell. Andrew got onto the helicopter with ease.

Once inside, I noticed a sign of relief on my parents' faces. But the one on my mother's face told me she wouldn't be letting me out of her sight for a long time. Then, of course, there was Andrew who wanted to do the entire thing all over again.

Oranges

Abigail R.

Oranges are so yummy, oranges are so cooling,
Juice is squirting out, I think I may be drooling.
Now I am peeling, now I am squealing,
For the yummy taste inside.
Oranges are so orange, the only fruit it's true,
Taking its name by its beautiful hue.
Oranges are round and weigh half a pound,
With a leathery skin outside.
Oranges are sweet, and sometimes sour,
They grow from a pretty white flower.
I love them so much, by their taste and their touch,
That I'll chase them the whole worldwide.

~

Sisters at Dance

Alexis S.

Dance! Dance! Dance! That's all Jessie wants to do. Jessie is 10 and she has 3 sisters. There is Maddie, Allie, and Sammie. Maddie is 9 years old, Allie is 10, and Sammie is 12. Allie is Jessie's twin sister. Jessie's sisters dance too. They dance at Dance Pink. All four of them are amazing dancers and all they want to do is dance.

All four sisters went to dance on Saturday morning. Jessie's ankle was hurting her so bad. Jessie's ankle normally hurts a little bit, but today it hurt very badly. Kianna always tells Jessie to dance through the pain in her ankle. Kianna is Jessie's dance teacher. Kianna told Jessie to tell her mom that her ankle hurts, but she did.

That Saturday, Jessie was doing a split jump and landed on her ankle funny. It hurt so bad that she started to cry. Her mom and all of her sisters saw through the window that she was crying and ran into the dance room. Her mom took Jessie to the hospital immediately. She was at the hospital for hours. The doctors said her ankle was hurt badly. It was broken.

Jessie loves pink. So when she got the cast, it was pink, but her cast was only up to her knee. During her time recuperating her ankle she went to the dance studio to watch and see what was going on with her classes. She thought it was great for her to watch her classes even though she couldn't dance!

Jessie finally got her cast off and was really excited to be able to dance again! She was a stronger dancer because her ankle was fixed. It turned out that before she broke her ankle there was a little scratch on the bone and that is why it had hurt so bad before!

Jessie's sisters are very happy that they all can dance together again.

~

There is a girl and she can fly

Ananya S.

In the town of things gone by there is a girl and she can fly
Over the treetops and mountains high there is a girl and she can fly
Soaring with birds in the ever blue sky there is a girl and she can fly
Doing things we wouldn't dare try there is a girl and she can fly
Smelling sweet fragrances up oh so high there is a girl and she can fly
Twirling and whirling as clouds pass by there is a girl and she can fly
A Passing, floating, drifting child there is a girl and she can fly
Staying up top for a quite long while there is a girl and she can fly
Yes, in the town of things gone by they rally with a deafening cry—
"In our town of things gone by we have a girl and she can fly!"

~

The Treacherous Mountain

Andrew K.

What a glorious day to climb a mountain, it was clear and sunny. Austria was so beautiful with all its glistening lakes and steep mountains.

When my neighbor, Chris, and I arrived at the mountain, I glanced up and it looked like the mountain was never going to end. I didn't like the look of the mountain. It was really steep and I'm afraid of heights. Plus we didn't bring any ropes or harnesses.

Chris was a seasoned climber with great instincts. I thought about climbing the mountain, thinking of all the other climbers who attempted this and failed and the 99.5 % chance of dying. But suddenly I came to a conclusion. Let's do this! As you can see I am fearless.

After about three hours of climbing, we were halfway up the mountain and it started to get foggy. At a ledge, we took a little break and planned our next route up the side of the mountain.

The most technically challenging part was next. "Hey Chris, it might get a little rough up here," I said.

"OK," Chris replied as he trailed behind me,

I was nervous and growing tired. I reached for a rock, and when my hand had a firm grip on it, I tried to pull myself up. But the rock slipped, and I was left dangling by one hand. I tried not to look down as I heard the rock bouncing down thousands of feet to the valley.

"You OK Andrew? I can't see a thing but I heard rocks falling," Chris yelled.

"I don't think you want to see anything," I replied. My heart was beating a thousand beats per minute and my hand was sweating like mad! Chris was too far away to help. After about a minute, my hand became tired and it slipped again. I saw a ledge below me and I used my quick reflexes to grab it. My heart was still pounding. Wow I couldn't believe I was still alive.

I took some time to think before I made my next move. Fortunately, the rest of the mountain wasn't so hard to climb. But just as we were going to take another break close to the top of the mountain, I glanced up to see how much further we had left to climb. Up ahead, I saw what appeared to be a large cat, light and dark gray in color, with pointy ears and sharp fangs. I could see him drooling.

It was really foggy but I recognized it as a lynx, and he was staring right at us. He appeared to be really skinny, like he hadn't eaten in a while so I thought we were going to be lunch. I whispered, "I think we should stay still and hope he goes away."

The lynx's yellow evil looking eyes were still staring at us and its balancing skills were amazing. Suddenly it darted down the mountain wall....but not at us. Apparently there was a mountain goat behind us and before you could say run, the goat was being crushed in the lynx's mouth.

Luckily, the rest of the mountain was an easy climb and we made it to the top about 30 minutes after the lynx incident. At the top we had a glorious view. It looked like we could see the entire country of Austria. We took pictures and sent them to Facebook (thank goodness for satellite).

Chris and I also packed fireworks to shoot off if we made it to the peak of the mountain. Before we shot off the fireworks, we had a couple of refreshing power drinks and talked about what mountain we should climb next.

We waited till it was dark to shoot off the fireworks so it would light up the sky for people to watch. Then we had a countdown "5.....
..4......3.......2........1........ we did it!!" we both shouted. The fireworks lit up the night sky. All the citizens far below us ran out of their houses to see what was going on. It was true, we made it!

~

A Singing Dream

Angela S.

"Deep breaths, deep breaths." Kylie kept thinking. "You got this, you're fine." she said silently. It was the Fall Festival Talent Show, and Kylie was about to sing the song she wrote. Everyone was going to watch her, even Stephanie. Stephanie used to be Kylie's best friend, but now she always has a mean comment for any of Kylie's songs. Stephanie has a grudge against Kylie, but it hasn't always been that way.

"Okay Kylie, just sing your heart out, and you'll be great." her mom said. Kylie nodded then stepped out onto the stage, and the lights immediately shined brightly on her, she took a deep breath then sang: "You think that I got everything good and all is straying my way. Figured I got everything, and always got a say...well, you're wrong, so wrong, but you still think ...that I think, that I am better than you, but you should know, that isn't true...we're the same , just me and you... so get on out of that seat, and join me singing this beat, Stephanie." Kylie looked towards Stephanie's seat, to see she wasn't there. Suddenly, Kylie felt a poke on the shoulder, and turned around to see a smiling Stephanie standing right beside her. "Let's do this, Kyle's." Stephanie said. "Only if you can keep up with me, Steph." Kylie said back with a grin. "We're equal you and I, and together we can fly.... we're equal you and I. Together we will fly, we're equal, you and I....." they sang in unison.

"Did you write that song for me?" Stephanie asked, eyes brimming with tears. "Actually, I wrote it about and for the both of us." Kylie responded, "By the way, why have you hated me since, like, the third grade? I mean, I never did anything horrible to you." "Do you remember the third grade Pro- Arts Day?" Stephanie asked. Kylie shook her head in confusion. "Well, we both were chosen to sing off of one of those song sheets on the table, and we chose the same one." "Oh yea, I remember that." Kylie commented. "If you can remember that, you must remember when it turned into a singing competition, you ending up winning, and the entire class ended up laughing at me, while you just stood there and smiled." Stephanie said in agony. "I never realized how upset you were about that, I never meant to hurt your feelings." Kylie said. "I just want us to be friends again." "You really mean that?" Stephanie asked, hopefully. "Of course I do." Kylie responded "Sure, I guess we can be friends. Oh, wipe that hurt look off your face, I miss you and want to be your friend again." Stephanie added, smiling.

That was the day, when they turned an old memory into a new song, and created a new future full of friendship.

The End

The Best New Year's Eve Ever

Ashley M.

Crack! Boom! Pop! Pop! Pop!

It was New Year's Eve, and everyone, I mean EVERYONE, in Bridgewater was at the New Year's festival that was held by the Rotary Club every year. The celebration took place in the heart of the town where all the best restaurants were.

It was a fact that all the people of Bridgewater were excited for the new year to begin. Sounds of excitement filled the air! Policemen were whistling on their newly polished silver whistles, telling people when to cross the town square. Shiny gold horns were tooted by small children, excited for the new year to begin. Melodious voices were heard from the 5th grade chorus, singing Auld Lang Syne while being conducted by Mrs. Lighthall. She was leading her students to sing to the crescent moonlight.

Everyone had a fresh bowl of yellow, greasy popcorn in their hands. Some crunched or munched, and others threw their popcorn in the air. As people were waiting for the New Year's countdown to begin, they played fun carnival games funded by the community, like a lollipop pyramid, bowling, and even a horseshoe toss. Everyone wanted to get a chance to hold the famous horseshoe from 1820. There were art projects to be started like making a New Year's flag, and sports to be played like soccer and kickball. There was even a hundred dollar lottery for whoever guessed the lucky number!

That's not all. There was also ice skating, which a lot of people never tried because it's always too hot in Bridgewater. A special type of plastic was used so now the members of Bridgewater could try out ice skating. This was such a hit, but unfortunately there weren't enough skates to go around so a gang of teenage boys tried to walk on they ice which ended up with two ambulances. It was an exciting, memorable experience to everyone.

Despite all the games and fun people were having, they all had their eyes on one thing: the huge, shimmering Christmas tree. The big, twinkling gold star on top of the tree looked like an angel from heaven. The Christmas tree was bigger than most people had ever seen. Some people said it was as big as two airplanes stacked end to end with a cherry on top. The colored lights glimmered against the pitch black sky. People picked out their favorite ornaments to decorate the Christmas tree with. Thanks to all the volunteers and the Rotary Club, the New Years was as splendid success.

All the people at the party were standing around the tree, chatting and talking about what presents they got for the holidays and to catch up with the latest news. Couples walked hand in hand underneath the midnight sky.

By now, kids were overwhelmed with all the games and fun things to do. They had never seen so many activities. Meanwhile the parents were running around like a chicken without a head, trying to chase their children all around to keep up with all the fun. By now, everyone was waiting impatiently for the New Year's countdown to begin.

As it got closer and closer to the time when the old year would cease to exist, people were frantically looking to get their families and friends together. Young girls ran to their crushes to be sure to get their picture perfect New Year's kiss. All eyes were turned to the gigantic grandfather clock, which stood proudly on a pedestal in the town square. The ticking of the clock got slower by the second. Finally, it was time to start.

Lights! Camera! Action!!!!! And the countdown began...

10...just starting!

9...now everyone was counting.

8...the clock ticked even faster.

7...woo! People started to cheer.

6...all eyes were glued to the night sky.

5...halfway to New Years.

4...almost there.

3...the din of the crowd was incredible.

2...time was coming near.
1!!!!!!!!!!!!!!!

Cheers of laughter and excitement filled the air. Popcorn and confetti were pouring tremendously from the colorful sky. The fireworks... oh, the fireworks! They filled the air with splendid shapes and colors of the rainbow. The audience was hypnotized by the sensational booms and explosions of the fireworks.

All the people in Bridgewater were excited for the new year to finally begin and all the new surprises that sat waiting ahead. Even the police put down their silver whistles to let the fireworks reflect upon them. Children were tooting their horns wildly while proudly waving their New Year's flags. They were trying to hold them up over the towering crowd. Mrs. Lighthall's 5th grade chorus was enchanted by the colorful wonders that lit up the night sky. The crowd cheered louder and louder and the fireworks got faster and faster.

Finally, the grand finale was finished and the smoke gradually dissolved into the darkness above. Popcorn, voices, and confetti were now coming to an end. The people of Bridgewater were started yawn after the day's excitement was gone. Mothers and fathers were carrying helpless, sleepy children to the car who were now dreaming about the fun that the next year would hold.

People were waving goodbye to their friends. Light by light, the Christmas tree faded into the night sky.

This is a FACT...this was the best New Year's Eve ever!

~

The Bully

August G.

Abby didn't want to go to school on her birthday. She didn't even want to go to school anymore! The new girl Amanda was always picking on her. She ruined every single day for her. But what could she do? Hide all day? She was actually thinking about doing that. Amanda was a bully to her, and nobody else.

One day at lunch, Abby faced her fears. She came up to Amanda and asked her why she only picks on her, and told her that she shouldn't pick on people at all. As Amanda turned around she slowly started to grin, "I only pick on you because I don't like your student council ideas." she said, but she lied. Out loud she said "I pick on you because I don't like your ideas" but in her head she was saying "I only pick on you because I'm jealous of you". I guess that's why bullies pick on others, or maybe it's just Amanda's reason. But let's get back to the story.

All night Abby thought about Amanda's words. All night she kept hearing, "I only pick on you because I don't like your ideas." "BUT THAT CAN'T BE RIGHT! I KNOW IT'S A LIE!" Abby yelled after repeating Amanda's words in her head for about 5 minutes. She never lied in her whole life and she can feel when someone is lying to her.

She came up to Amanda at recess and started shouting "TELL ME THE TRUTH ABOUT WHY YOU PICK ON ME!" Amanda shyly looked up at her and said "Okay, I'll tell you." she said. Amanda took a deep breath and said "I'm jealous, I'm jealous of how you look, and your amazing ideas. I'm just jealous of you." "Well why didn't you tell me before? We could have been great friends if you would've told me the truth." said Abby. "Yea, I guess that would've been better." replied Amanda. "Wanna start over?" asked Abby. "Yea, I'd like that, and thanks for forgiving me." They both smiled and walked away. And so, they became friends. But not just any friends, BEST FRIENDS!

The Search for King Spock: The Rocky Chambers, Book One

Benjamin P.

CHAPTER ONE

It didn't all start on a dark, spooky night. Actually, it started on a sunny morning in a small village. I'm Brock Starburst. Everyone loves my last name.

I am not the only one who doesn't know why the big wall on one side of the village is there. People say it was built to help our village, but I don't see how it helps in any way. Whoever built it must have been a lunatic, because now every single child in the village, including me, who wonders what is on the other side has no way of finding out. Until today.

But now I wish I had never known.

Anyway, I was heading over to my friend Tommy Pillbister's house to see the remodeling that they had recently got.

Wow, this house was shiny! The dining room glittered. Even the sheet covering the wooden table glistened. My friend showed me around the house. The rest of it was just as amazing; everything as shiny as a golden trophy.

Tommy was a great artist. He and I were both very brave. That might have been our only chance of saving the village, because for our journey, bravery was what we needed most.

As I went up the stairs to the top floor, I remembered his room. Ever since I had been told not to go in there, I had made several attempts to see it but failed every time. Now, if he was too busy stalking around the house and talking about the remodeling to look back, maybe I could sneak away.

I raced down the hall and pulled at the doorknob. Someone was pulling at the other end!

"Whoever's there, let go! Oh, is that you, Brock? Let me out!"

"No, mom." I replied in my best Tommy voice. "It's me, Tommy. I was just going to lock the door." I didn't want her to know it really was me.

"Oh, I'll do it now. Go back and play with Brock." "Okay." I ran off toward Tommy.

Surprisingly, he was still talking. "Blah blah and then the remodeler came and blah blah and drilled into blah blah, but when I blah blah, it was blah blah. So then there was a hole, and blah blah. We had to push a special blah blah so it could stay, but we had to blah blah with it too. It finally blah blah to make out the little blah blah, but then it stuck to the blah blah. We had to blah blah to get it out. The blah blah was steady now, so blah blah took tweezers and blah blah. Can you believe that?! He needed to use tweezers!"

Tweezers. Amazing.

I have to admit that sometimes Tommy can be a little boring. I wondered if he was ever going to get to the end of his story. There was a very unlikely chance. But sometimes things may seem unlikely but actually happen. For example, it was unlikely that me and Tommy would survive our quest. But you never know, you never know.

The car ride home seemed like hours because Tommy kept on yakking away. (It was only ten minutes, though.) I think even his mother was getting a little annoyed. His words now seemed like a pattern. Blah yak blah yak blah yak.

When I got home I plopped down on the couch after telling my mom, "Hello." You may or may not like the show "The Tunnels of Doom." It is about a boy who gets trapped in a variety of secret tunnels and has to find an exit and avoid obstacles.

This episode, the boy, Shaun, finds the jewel of healing. When he takes it, a giant boulder breaks the ground and he falls into a trap. He rips through the net he is caught in and finds a passage that leads to-to-to-TO BE CONTINUED shows up on the screen.

"No!" I cried. "Come on, this season the episodes end at all the good parts! Jeez, who were the creators of this show? They don't know when to end it!"

I pointed the remote at the TV to see the other recordings that I had, but then NO SIGNAL also showed up on the screen after I deleted "The Tunnels of Doom."

"Pfffft. Mom, this show had a virus and now 'no signal' is bouncing around the screen. Just like it does for Samsung when you have the screen paused for too long."

"Okay, I'll try my best. You know I'm not as good as your dad when it comes to TV. But maybe I can do it. Go outside and play, Brock. It's a nice day, and probably the only one for a while." My mom called back down to me. So I trudged down the porch in our backyard. I didn't know what to do.

I couldn't go to Tommy's, because I was just there. But I could get my Moon Shoes from the garage and jump the fence, as I sometimes did. And I noticed that, for the first time ever, my grumpy neighbors were not home, and they could not catch me jumping their fence, as they always did.

I bounced for a bit, then I was ready for takeoff. I shot through the air like a bullet. It was in the air that I realized the straps on my Moon Shoes had not been strapped in tight. My bouncing shoes fell to the ground as I flew over the fence. I hit my elbow when I hit the ground, but I was alright. It could have been a lot worse. But then I realized it was a lot worse. I was trapped in my always-angry neighbors' backyard!

You can get out of this. Be a man, Brock!

Those were my only thoughts before I started yelling for help. Then, a minute later, I heard an engine. Mr. Tarkenson slid open the back door. I was busted.

"Come with me!!!" He demanded. He squeezed my arm tight and pulled me through the house to wherever he was taking me. He pointed to the ground on the side of his house where the Moon Shoes had fallen.

"One more time, sonny, and I'm keeping yer shoes and yee will never get them shoes back! Yee got that, sonny? Yee got that?"

"I got that." I moaned.

The rest of the day went by very quickly. Before I knew it, I was in bed, and half-asleep. I wasn't fully asleep because I was too busy worrying about the old man's words. One more time, sonny, and I'm keeping yer shoes and yee will never get them shoes back!

I decided not to worry. I just had to make sure my shoes were strapped in tighter than before. So then I would be able to bounce straight back if the Tarkensons were coming. Then, tiredly, I closed my eyes shut.

The next morning I was awoken by a strange DINGA-DINGA from below. It sounded like a buzz and a ding at the same time. I hurried downstairs, still in my pajamas.

I peeked through the peephole and there was Tommy, as unpredictable as ever.

"What are you doing here? It's six thirty! Why are you up? You have rings at the bottom of your eyes. Go home and get more sleep! I need more also." I really wasn't that tired, but I wanted Tommy to go back home.

"No, I'm not letting you go back to sleep until you see this." Tommy replied. With that, he pulled the unlocked door open and tugged me all the way to the wall at the end of the village.

"Look at this, it's amazing." He bent down on one knee and swiped his hand against the gray wall. It revealed a line down the wall that was about three inches tall.

"What?!" I cried. Never before had there been a single dent in the wall. A little clank made both me and Tommy jump back in horror. A sharp-pointed silver spear-shaped object dug its way through.

"Ahhhhhhh!" Me and Tommy stumbled back, and I collapsed on top of him. We were both too scared to speak. What was that?

I didn't speak to Tommy for a week. I was too mad at him for bringing me to that spooky sight. Plus, he had made me afraid of the wall breaking down even though that was what I had always wanted to happen. And it got me into a whole lot of trouble when it did break down.

Basically, I did most of the work on our journey and got into the most danger for doing that. Tommy really didn't help out. He was always complaining and every time it would be a different complaint. The stupidest complaint was that he was too cold.

And right now I was just standing around in gym class at school, and Tommy was having a leg ache. At least that was what he told Mr. Preston.

Still, at some parts of our journey, if Tommy wasn't around to help, I would have been toast. So actually, I am thankful that he is my friend.

Mr. Preston wasn't just going to let Tommy off so easily. He never did to anyone. "Go to the nurse! If it isn't broken, you play! And if you keep acting so babyish, I will make sure to give you the worst grade possible for gym on your report card!"

Tommy stood there, open-mouthed. So did I.

A punishment like that was the worst the gym teacher could do. Poor Tommy.

I had had enough of that gym teacher. I ran up to him. "You deserve this!" And I punched his face. He stumbled back and hit his laptop that was playing a Rocky song and his speakers. The speakers smashed to the ground and then so did the laptop. The Rocky song abruptly stopped. A power cord cut open at the force of the laptop, the speakers, and the teacher himself. Sparks shot out, then the lights flickered and went out.

Everyone cheered. But then I heard a click behind me. Uh oh. Mrs. Sacharotto, the principal, had her flashlight pointed at me.

"Mr. Starburst, what happened here?! We heard a crash and I came running down here! What is this all about?!"

"Well, Mr. Preston started running around the room and trying to trample us! So I had no choice but to punch him! He hit the power cord and the lights went out in here!"

"Ahhh, well, usually punching isn't allowed, but since it was an emergency, you aren't in trouble. Mr. Preston, on the other hand, will be fired. I will get you all out of here safely and then you must get back to class quickly." Yes! I couldn't figure out how she believed me, but she did!

Later that day I strapped my Moon Shoes in tight and jumped the fence. It worked out perfectly. I was having a great day. I was sure it couldn't get better. But it did.

Ronald Crifton, the school bully, had actually wanted to come over to my house to "hang out" with me! I guess even he didn't like mean old Preston!

Even though I was now being a popular kid for beating up the guy, I was still afraid of Ronald. I didn't want to take any chances of being beat up just like the now-fired gym teacher.

I could still "hang out" with other kids that liked me. Just not Ronald Crifton.

I went to bed that night thinking about what I did. I never knew I had enough power in my punches to knock the strong teacher over. He probably had a muscle in every bone. Maybe even in his brain, although brains don't have bones.

His brain is probably going "Look at my biceps!" over and over and over again. I laughed at this thought. And with that, I fell asleep.

In the morning I woke up and did my daily schedule before school. As I walked out the front door, I heard a loud BOOM that made me half deaf for a minute. That was why a big CRASH from the wall only sounded like a peep to me.

But I knew at that moment that something was wrong. So I took off.

By the time I got to the wall I could hear fully again. And I could hear screams of people I knew while people I didn't know carried them away. A group of people that looked plain evil were heading my way, so I ducked behind some trees. I scurried closer and closer to the wall, hiding behind the trees as I went. I could see a mansion up ahead. It was clearly past our side of the wall. Then I saw Tommy being carried away. I remembered my strong arm and hand and chucked a rock at the evil kidnapper. Tommy came up to me. I had freed Tommy, and now I needed to find out what was going on.

TO BE CONTINUED...

Party Balloon Man

Bradley L.

One day Jon and his mom were looking for a balloon. They were at Party City. "There are many to choose from," said the store clerk. There was a huge wall filled with balloons, but one in particular caught his eye. It was a medium sized balloon, with a huge face including eyes, nose, and a mouth, and in huge red and green letters it read: "LETS PARTY!" Jon was really fascinated by it. He begged at his mom's side for it, but every time he tried, he couldn't convince her. Then he said "I know why we should get it. It is a very special and unusual balloon!" He must have persuaded her because all of a sudden, Jon's mom said, "ok, we will buy it." The balloon cost $20. Jon's mom asked the clerk to get it down and then Jon's mom paid for it. Jon was jumping for joy! He couldn't wait for tomorrow!

On the day of the party, Jon woke up with a smile on his face. He was so happy about the party! But as he was walking downstairs for breakfast, he heard very strange noises. To Jon, it sounded like "eei, eei, eei, eei." Jon wondered what is was, but he didn't let it bother him. Jon's mom made him a fabulous breakfast. It was chocolate chip pancakes, with maple syrup and bacon. That was his favorite breakfast in the whole world. Still, the noise continued. Jon was really getting bothered by it. The party was now only an hour away. Jon was so excited he thought he was going to die, but he hoped the noise would stop by the start of the party. If not, he thought his party would be ruined, and he could not accept that. All his friends would make fun of him. That would be a total nightmare!

The party was now 15 minutes away. Jon was super excited! But the noise still continued. As the first guest arrived, the noise got even louder. It was Jon's best friend arriving. His name was Tim. As the second guest arrived, the noise grew even more. Now, as the third guest arrived something really strange happened. The noise had changed to “oo oo oo” As all of the guests had arrived, something extremely odd had happened. As Jon’s mom was serving snacks, something had jumped out of the balloon. To Jon, it looked like a person. It reached for the snacks and ate them all. Jon thought it was crazy. His worst nightmare was coming true! All the kids at school would tease him! But Jon had the courage to ask it what it was. He asked it, “Hello stranger. Why are you here today?” Jon wasn’t expecting an answer, but he got one. The reply was, “Hello. My name is Party Balloon Man, P.B.M. for short. You know your balloon? I was inside it. I come out for every party. And those noises, I was making them because I was so excited for your party. I am deeply sorry, though.” Jon was shocked to hear that. He replied: “Oh. I forgive you. You can stay at my party.” “Really?” asked Party Balloon Man. “Sure” said Jon. He even gave P.B.M. cake and included him in the party games. The following day at school, all the kids told Jon they loved his party. Jon thought they were going to tease him, but they didn’t. Jon was amazed. And for as long as he lived, Jon kept Party Balloon Man in the balloon. And at every party he had, yes, P.B.M. came out and had a good time. And the kids didn’t like it—no, they loved it!!!!

THE END!!!!

Jennifer's Great Show

Bridget Z.

Jennifer Stone stuffed her books in her bag and swung her backpack over her shoulder. Then she raced outside to meet her best friend Lisa at the main entrance of Middleton Elementary School, where she was in 4th grade. She located her friend Lisa in the swarming crowd of students and ran up to her. Unlike Jennifer, Lisa was shy. "Hey." Lisa nearly whispered as Jennifer drew nearer. "C'mon Lisa, we have soccer practice today, right at 3:30. We have fifteen minutes to get there. By the way, what's with you today?" Jennifer hatched up a conversation as they began walking toward the soccer field. She hated when the walk to soccer was quiet. "Oh... it's just that I'm really bothered about the talent show coming up in two days." Lisa told Jennifer. "But you aren't doing an act, right? You told me you had stage fright earlier." questioned Jennifer. The two friends, Jennifer and Lisa, talked about the upcoming school talent show for the rest of the walk to practice. "I know I'm not in the show," said Lisa, "But I really wanted you sitting next to me, whispering funny things." "Don't worry Lisa, it won't be too lonely." Jennifer soothed. She thought to herself: Personally, I'm really excited for the song I'll be singing for the talent show, I can't wait! When they reached the soccer field, their team was already doing warm-up. Lisa and Jennifer joined in, kicking the ball around the cones. When Jennifer kicked the ball around the 3rd cone, she thought of the talent show. She started to feel bad for Lisa, because they'd always sat together during the school talent shows. Lost in thought, Jennifer tripped over a tree root jutting out of the grass. She fell to the ground. "Ouch!" Jennifer moaned "I think I twisted my ankle..." She knew then, that she would never be able to perform in the show. If Jennifer got a cast, which she knew she would get, it would look really ugly onstage, and Jennifer would rather not participate than go onstage all wobbly and in crutches. She knew she had no choice but not to be in the talent show. Two days later, Jennifer sat next to a-very-happy-Lisa during the school talent show, pretending to be happy, too. But deep in her heart, She wished to be up on stage performing, her lifetime wish. Would she ever get to perform the song she practiced so much? Suddenly, she hated her twisted ankle that took way too long to heal. She hated soccer. She hated Lisa. She hated everything. Couldn't life get better for her?!?! It turns out, yes. When two more months had passed, when her ankle had healed, her mother signed her up for the village hall talent show. Even better than a school talent show! Many more people would see her act. There were going to be more prizes and more fun! The song she'd been practicing seemed so babyish now. Jennifer had to think of a new act to do. Grander, she decided. Jennifer asked her mom for a ride to Lisa's house. She could never plan out the costume, song, and dance all by herself! Jennifer would have to ask Lisa for help. For the next few days until the village talent show, Jennifer rode to Lisa's house to plan out her act. It was nice of Lisa to help her, even if Lisa knew that Jennifer wouldn't be able to sit next to her during the show. Finally, at last, it was the day of the talent show. Jennifer waited backstage before her act. She sat on the floor, trembling in the backstage area, mumbling the words to her song. Jennifer's palms sweated, and someone walking past could easily see she was really nervous. The host of the show came through the curtains and called: "Jennifer S., it's your turn to perform, please come onstage." Jennifer climbed up to her feet, wiped her palms on the tights of the costume she and Lisa had designed, and walked onstage. She put on a nervous smile and said toward the audience: "Special thanks to Lisa M." She heard a gasp from the crowd and saw Lisa covering her mouth with her hands. Jennifer giggled to herself and began to sing and dance. As soon as she started, she never wanted to stop. She was even quite sad when the song ended and the villagers clapped and cheered loudly for her. She went back through the curtains and the host of the show went on. She announced into the microphone: "Ladies and gentlemen, now is time for the awards. In first place, Jennifer Stone! Please give a round of applause to Jennifer!" that was all Jennifer heard. Her mind began racing. She went back through the curtains and received her trophy. Then she greeted her parents as she got offstage. "There's got to be a picture for the winner!" her mother said. Lisa nodded in agreement, next to her parents. Jennifer's mom took out her camera. "Say cheese!" her mom said "One, two..." Jennifer grabbed Lisa by the arm and pulled Lisa next to herself, just as her mother shouted "Three!" Jennifer couldn't have done it without her. Lisa deserved to be in the picture, too.

~

Snow Day

Caimin X.

The word "snow day" means much more than the word "weekend" does to me because on snow day I get to wake up and get to go back to sleep again. I also have more time for homework and fun! On snow days I have a lot of fun by playing, sleeping, and doing homework. The best part of snow days is being able to do thing I usually don't get to do.

Waking up is not my favorite thing. Whenever my dad wakes me up on weekdays, I am very cranky and not in a good mood but if I have a snow day I can sleep as long as I want. Once I woke up at 9:00 a.m. and I got scared and worried because I had no idea that it was a snow day. Am I late for school? Soon I found out that it was a snow day by looking out the window: I saw so much snow piled on the sidewalk. I then happily went back to my cozy bed again and slept another 1 hour.

After I finally finish sleeping, I take time to move right along to the next thing. Piles of homework for me to do are all over my house, but I never get to do all of it or even any of it, because I like to get to my hubbies first such as soccer and dancing. On snow days I can do a lot of homework and can even take my time to do my best. Sometimes I enjoy rushing through all the homework, but other times I am stuck on one problem and it makes me mad and frustrated when it happens. Most of the time I am able to find out the answer and feel proud of myself.

When I am stuck on one problem and can't find the answer, I will take a break on homework and move on to playing so I won't be in a bad mood. I like making crafts and doing cartwheels for fun, but playing with my brother, Caiyi, is my most favorite. He is a great partner for the games because he never cheats. He is also very busy so I can't play with him all the time. On snow days he has more time to play after his homework. The fun breaks calm me down and bring me back to a good mood for homework.

Snow days are full of fun. When snow days finally come, I get to sleep in, which makes me in a good mood for the rest of the day. Working on piles of homework I never get to do at school makes me feel good about learning. The best part about snow days is when I get to have a lot of fun by playing in between homework. All of these reasons make snow day fun and enjoyable.

~

Disappearing Parents

Caiyi X.

To: The people that found my diary
From: Chris Jamesford
Date: 1/23/2012

Memoir: Days went past by without recondition from the small family, in Kansas City, people were disappearing every second but from whom? As I recall too that day: "Chris dinner is ready!" "Coming mom" I shouted back while climbing the small stairs to my collection of Lego's. I stacked up my Lego's piece by piece to form the Seven Wonders of the World. And that was maybe the last time I saw them in the years of my life. At that time I was only 4 years old.

Well that was in Kansas where my old house was, after my parents disappeared I fled the house to search for them across the globe had I finally traced them to one spot: Caracas, Venezuela.

....

May I introduce myself? My name is Chris Jamesford, now I am almost 17 years old, and I had been living without my parents. How I survived? As friends of both my parents boss took me in and then threw me out when I was bad. You may wonder do I have friends or family. Well I don't know. All I knew of my parent's origins were either taken with them or stolen. From that day on I have a mystery to solve.

Years ticked by like a bomb waiting for the right moment. My parents seemed human enough, acted like a human, did everything like a human. To me that did not flow—why did perfectly human parents disappear in the dead of the night?

....

Well you might think why don't you go back to Kansas and scour through the house. yes. I did do that, all I found was slim gray laptop, skinnier than an Ipad. I flipped it open; the dusty gray screen flickered to life. There was the picture of my parents at the Teen age standing and taking a pose. I saw a post-it note jutting out of a pile of yellowed with age papers I quickly picked up the fragile post-it note, it read:

Date: 3/12/1999
Meet me outside the window.
Signed: Patrick Goob
P.S. go to the international airport
then get a flight to Caracas, Venezuela
Reward would be: $400,000,000

That broke the last straw who ever persuaded my parents to abandon me, it had to be the money in scripted on the post-it note. I bet that my parents hid the note so I won't find it.

I decided to pack my bag straight away those included: a stolen semi -automatic Pistol, water, Ramen noodles, and 2 pairs of shoes, all into one black bag. I have to sneak every single one of my things in, there is no way that I am going to pass without me being checked and searched. I will have to think of a genius Idea.

Sooner or later I will have to create a fake passport, boarding pass, and a first class ticket.

End of Diary Entry #1

To: The people that found my diary
From: Chris Jamesford
Date: 1/25/2012

I fled to the airport as quick as I could on my feet so I wouldn't get caught by the police. In that operation it took me 2 days to accomplish 37 miles of road. And now I am stuck in the Kansas City international airport trying to sneak into a fight to Caracas, Venezuela.

I finally found a perfect flight nonstop flight to Cascara. I froze and looked at the screen it shows the flight number and time it said:

Flight Number: CAR 5.104
Departure time: 6:40 PM
Gate #: C-31
Flight Time: 8 hours

That finally turned my brain right now it was 6:29. I raced through the crowd of the densely populated airport, making my way into the gate. I bumped into a stout man similar to a Neanderthal, with a thick black beard a tall top hat like Abe Lincoln's own. Thoughts raced through my head. What should I say? I began to mumble things that I don't even know.

A wave of nausea hit me full force and that ring a bell in my head was he a weird kind of person that controlled people's mind like a magician? OR was he the man who did persuade my parents to abandon me?

....

I snuck past the security guards with a family that looked familiar to me. I crawled under all the electronics of the security guards and waited until they were on a coffee break, today I got really lucky passing the guards.

I thought of the first lie that came to my head.

I muttered like a slave to his master "Um... Excuse me sir may I ask for your name please? I am taking a survey of the most common first names in America."

I let out a huge sigh of relief when I was done.

The man I met returned "My name is Patrick Goob" After he finished he turned on his left heel and left.

That guy was the exact guilty guy who persuaded my parents to leave me. Flames boiled in my heart, just watching that man walk way innocently just makes me want to take out my pistol and shoot him straight in the back. I debated in my head as I ran in the opposite direction. I charged to the gate of the flight, I was very lucky NO ONE NOTICED ME! I took that row in the entire airplane so I wouldn't be so oblivious to the rest of the people.

I just wonder what is next

End of Diary Entry #2

To: The people that found my diary
From: Chris Jamesford
Date: 1/26/2012

As time ticked by slowly, I felt drowsy in a short notice of time. I forgot to bring a book or anything to keep my company, all I could do was fall asleep.

It has been 8 hours since I last wrote in my so called "Travel Journal AKA: Diary"

As I walked down the ramp of the Airplane my shoes touched the black staircase leading down to the Venezuelan soil. The sweet tropical sun kissed my blank white American face.

I walked slowly down the market covered street filled with hundreds of sun baked skinned people. The question is where are my parents staying? The sun beat down hard in my face; I squinted hard to strain on my vision. The main problem came into mind is where my parents are! I fumbled through my bag for something to do but the only thing that tumbled out was my stolen semi-automatic pistol. With that in the streets of Caracas it will attract many precocious citizens that are xenophobia about foreign people. I better be careful about this action/plan. At that moment a whole group of bandits started shouting something in Spanish, all I could make out was this *"¿qué quieres,¡Detente! ¡Detente! tú eres el que yo estoy buscando."*

I have seriously no idea what they are talking about. To me it sounds like American gibberish.

A sudden sharp pain in the thigh took the strength out of me and collapsed to the ground with a thud. Then things went all black for me.

....

It's been hours since I woke up in this dark and damp room, everything that I brought in hope of helping my parents escape was demolished. The pistol was filled with explosive bullets. The water was not special, the Ramen noodles were also explosive, the shoes bottom layer was a blade. DON'T ASK ME HOW I GOT THOSE COOL GADGETS!

Somebody is opening my cell door I better keep this out of their faces or this will be confiscated along with the other gadgets that they took.

I think it is the same exact people who took my parents, and now they are after me.

End of Diary Entry #3

I have to get out of here at any cost and find my parents that are what I came here to do. I have to shred every single piece of evidence in this place or I and my parents won't be safe, they would keep tracking us until they had us dead.

To: The people that found my diary
From: Chris Jamesford
Date: 1/27/2012

They took several tests on me when they took me out. I have no idea who and what they are doing. Their faces were covered heavily in black cloth. The testing room was filled with animals of all sorts in the middle where two cages stood side by side. Inside was a man in his 30's or 40's and a woman about the same age sitting hungrily in the middle of the cage. I really think those were my parents, the people who captured them made me parents unrecognizable so I wouldn't find out that they were here at all. I have to get them out. Along with that semi-impossible task I will have to call them Mom and dad to make sure that they really are my parents.

....

I think I saw my black backpack sitting against the wooden desk. I have to get the humans out of here if they are my parents or not. I picked up a gray stone perfect for throwing, the next time that the guards opened the doors I would throw the projectile at his\her face at full force. I looked upon the door to see if there is a way could get out but there is none, but a sign that says: *Organization: Blackjack, project: 67*.

....

I somehow had to get my parents out and end the *Organization: blackjack*.

The waiting is finally over the door finally started to click open, I got ready to throw then BAM! The guard was down in a split second. I picked up the stone on the way because that was the only weapon I had. This is similar to a do or die mission. I dashed around to the animal cages bashing every cage lock open as I ran around like a wild man. Until I came to the man cages I said "Mom, Dad?"

"Yes, Chris we were waiting for you, you have grown a lot son." Mom said "Don't you worry I will get you out of this mess and go home and be a full family together."

The guards are coming I heard their heavy footsteps on the marble floor. I finally bring myself to smash the locks of their cages. Thick skinned hands grabbed my shoulders; I smashed the rock into his hand. He screamed and fell back in shock. The animals were devouring the guards bit by bit or organ by organ.

I grabbed my birth parents and ran for my life to the exit while all the animals are on a killing spree. I thought to the guards. That is what you guys deserve for not feeding the animals at all. Everything ends here, the organization Blackjack destroyed there is no way that we are ever separating our family.

....

We fled onto the airplane the same way that I did and flew back to Kansas, moved back into our old house. I just hope everything that my parents have gone through will be nothing but an old memory chip. This will be the last diary entry for me to write in this journal.

Everything will be normal, like a regular American family, spending time together for 17 years not to be away for 13 years and not seeing anyone but animals. That is just not what a family is made to do.

I will have to put this away for the good of our reunited family, after being 13 years apart from each other. There is no way that me and my families are separating ever again, and we will remain a family until the end of time.

End of Diary Entry # 4, and the Final.

The Greatest Treasure

Camron M.

CHAPTER ONE

"Come on James we have to go to the airport" Theo shouted. "Coming Theo" James said in a harsh tone. Theo and James were both college students from The University of Chicago. Theo was a thin young man who was always in a hurry. James was also skinny, but very relaxed. They were headed to the O'Hare airport in Chicago, Illinois. They heard about a newly discovered artifact in San Sebastian, Peru. They were going to one of the most remote parts of Peru to investigate. As Theo and James made their way out of their college dorm room, they heard an odd sound. They looked at each other, ignored it, and left to catch a cab.

The driver wore a red Chicago Bulls cap with a black hoody. He talked in a Chicago accent and was African-American. He asked "What is your destination, sirs?" Theo and James said "O'Hare," at almost the same time. The driver then asked "which terminal?" Theo murmured "international," and they proceeded on their journey. They had a short conversation with the taxi driver about what a nice car he had.

Once they arrived at the O'Hare airport, Theo paid the driver and thanked him. They went to check in all their bulky bags. The lady that checked their bags had an American Airlines uniform with a blue tailored skirt. Later, they proceeded to an area and filled out their visa forms. By noon, they were on the airplane flying high in first class. The University was paying for their entire trip.

It was a long exhausting flight to Peru, but they were lucky because it was a direct flight. After a grueling night of traveling they had finally arrived at the Jorge Chávez International Airport. From there, it was a pleasant five-hour car ride. During the entire five hours, they were talking about this artifact that could supposedly convert everyday items into gold. But for a brief time they spoke to the driver.

The cab driver was a Latino man with black hair who spoke Spanish. They could only slightly communicate with him because Theo knew a little Spanish.

Once they arrived in San Sebastian, they couldn't wait to get their hands on the artifact. When they saw it, they weren't that impressed. It was just a box with cryptic writing on it. They approached a frenzied scientist, wearing a green plaid jacket and faded jeans. "Does this work?" they asked him. He admitted he did not know. If his theory was correct, they needed to unlock the box to get their hands on the actual artifact, the greatest treasure of all. So Theo asked "where is the key?" The scientist mumbled that he didn't know. James said "awe great, we came all this way so you could tell us we need to find a key." "No," he replied "you came to San Sebastian so we could tell you we need your help finding the key."

TO BE CONTINUED...

The Lion Kingdom

Carlos F.

Once upon a time there was a peaceful kingdom named Lion Kingdom. A powerful king named Francis ruled it. King Francis was well-respected and loved by his people. Lion Kingdom had many rivers, lakes, prairies and beautiful mountains. Most people farmed, some traded and fished for their living. The people lived in harmony.

But one day, a big and evil dragon came and attacked the kingdom. It burned the farms and houses. The next day, it came back to bring more destruction to the kingdom. The people were very terrified by the dragon. The King evacuated his people by the river. The King and his people went by the river because it was a bit far from the battle.

The next day the battle began. It was a very dangerous fight. The dragon can burn anything in its path and uses its sharp claws to harm people. Many of the soldiers died. The dragon escaped.

King Francis sends out three brave men named Jason, Wolfgang and Diego to hunt and kill the dragon. Jason was King Francis' son and was a great soldier. Wolfgang was adventurous and a very daring soldier. Diego was a wise, veteran soldier and a very good map-reader.

Before the three soldiers went to battle, King Francis led them to pray for protection. King Francis gave them weapons, food and tools. King Francis led them to the boat. The boat was not very big. It had a big deck. Inside, there were three comfortable beds. It also had big cannons on the side.

They travelled to the island were the dragon lived. It was not easy, they passed through dangerous storms, and big waves almost swept their boat.

When they reached the island, they saw a big forest. When they entered the forest, they were so surprised that there are no animals around. There were no animals because the dragon ate all the animals and some also got burned. The dragon was evil because his parents thought him to hate humans. The dragons saw that the humans killed the dragons for their skin.

The three soldiers know how mean the dragon is. They know they cannot defeat him when he is awake. Diego, being the wise one, suggested that they should attack the dragon when it is already sleeping.

When night came, they heard a loud snore, Zzzzzzzzzz!!! The three soldiers knew it was the dragon. They followed where the sound was coming from. Yes, it was the dragon! They took out their swords quietly and together they cut out the dragons' head.

They finally returned back to Lion Kingdom victoriously. The King and his people offered a prayer of thanksgiving and there was a great feast.

~

My Worst Day of Camp

Caroline B.

"Ukkk! Why does it have to start raining in the middle of a hike!" I exclaimed.

My friend, Ana, and I were with our camp troop at Camp Running Water in the center of the woods and it just started to drizzle. All that did was add humidity to an already sticky day.

Amanda, our counselor, said to watch out for bugs and poisonous plants, so I glanced quickly around at the trees. By now everyone was damp and annoyed but no one complained. At the moment it didn't look like we'd finish the hike, then again no human can predict nature exactly.

All of a sudden, rain pelted down like bullets and everyone was drenched in seconds. Amanda kept us trudging through the rain.

THWACK! BANG! CRASH! Ana and I happened to be in the back of the group but we didn't need to see to know what was going on. Judging by everyone's sudden stop and some frantic screams, it was all too obvious a tree had been struck by lightening and fallen nearby, blocking our path.

I pushed through the crowd to see Amanda screaming loudest of all; she was even hyperventilating. Now I was positive this hike was not going to go on much longer. Then even more unexpectedly, in the blink of an eye, Amanda broke into a sprint seemingly at the speed of light, down the trail, leapt over the fallen tree and kept running out of sight. We campers were now on our own and everyone stared at Ana and I.

" We'll never get out of here!" Kylie screamed wailing. "We're doomed."

"Stop thinking like a pessimist," I hissed, " We'll never get out of here if you don't want to."

“We’ll be able to get out of here if we try,” Ana agreed. She always thinks like an optimist when we need it most.

“Why don’t you two get us out of here then, you’re the nature freaks anyway”

“Yeah, you two know the trails better than anyone here,” one of Kylie’s friends chimed in.

“We’ll do it,” we both replied at once.

Neither of us were sure what to do, seeing as we’d never led a hike in the middle of a severe thunder storm before and certainly never planned to. Especially when our counselor had just had a severe meltdown and ran off to who knows where. Then since we had no other option, we led the group back on through the rain towards our cabins.

An ecstatic surge off accomplishment ran through me the moment we got the group back safely, but it didn’t last long. My emotions immediately turned to terrified when something electric and and neon yellow flashed past my eyes. THWAM! the cabin spilt in half!

“Eeek,” I whimpered unable to speak in fear.

“Did our cabin just get struck by lightening?” Ana squeaked clearly as terrified as me.

“I think so,” I responded finding my voice, but no less frightened. “Let’s get out of here before a fire starts.”

“C’mon, creek?” she stammered pointing towards the the flooded stream. We stood for a second trying to decide what to do. Soon enough we saw an odd red and orange glow coming from our cabin that felt like an odd heat wave.

“Yep fire, What do we do?” I asked Ana my face going pale. We thought for a minute and then I saw the answer.

“ Pump right there, bucket floating downstream, can you get it?” I asked.

“Sure,” Ana dove for the bucket, missed it, dove again and grabbed it just before the current took it out of her reach. “Got it”

We took turns pumping, then dashing to dump the water on the fire. Five long minutes later in front of us was a throughly burned down cabin, a smoldering fire and our legs felt like lead. We took the last bucket together, so exhausted we could barely carry it.

By nightfall, the fire was out and the adults rushed over to congratulate us on our intrepid and mature behavior. The next day we left Camp Running Water with a scary but amazing memory that we will cherish forever. We even get to come back next year and rebuild the cabin that was struck by lightening, split in half and burned down.

~

Lunchables

Charles Z.

Hi! My name is Charles Z. I am writing about a story called "Lunchables".

It starts one day when kids named Preston White, Mark Twins, and Cassidy White, were walking to Mark's house to play. "Now I am going to tell the characteristics about the 3 of them". Preston White was Cassidy's brother and he was the most talkative. Mark Twins was the smartest, but not the strongest. Cassidy White, also known as Preston's sister, was very strong. Now, where was I? Oh yes. All of them were walking down the street to Mark's house to play, when Cassidy said: Is someone whispering?

Um... Preston began to speak, it was me. He said, I was the one whispering.

What were you whispering about? Mark asked.

Lunch. Why lunch? Cassidy asked.

Preston said: It's lunch because I can't decide what lunch to bring on the fieldtrip to the Shedd aquarium. Mark asked: What's the matter with that?

That means I can't have lunch, Preston said.

What? Mark asked.

Yep, Preston said.

Then, Cassidy said: Why doesn't your mom pick?

She doesn't pick on my business, Preston said. I've tried terriaki chicken with broccoli, egg sandwhich, and tomato sandwhich.

Cassidy said: Wait, what about salad?

Preston said: Too crunchy.

How about your own? Mark said.

I don't like mine. Wait, what about Lunchables? Cassidy asked.

Preston asked: Which one? Pizza. Hmmm....You know what? You're right. I'll ask my mom to buy that one.

Suddenly, Mark's watch rang. It said it was time to go home, so they went to the door and waved bye.

The end

The Fright of the Roller Coaster

Cheryl C.

"STOP!" I yelled. Ever since my sister received the Six Flags flyer in the mail, she'd been bugging me all weekend about going to Six Flags, a roller coaster park.

"Stop, Stop, STOP!" I yelled. "You know I hate roller coasters.''

"Come on chicken, it's not like you'll die," protested my sister. My sister held up a fist. Usually I was scared but not today.

"Maybe I will, you never know," I shouted. I threw the pillow I was holding at her, even though I wanted to shatter a cup on her head.

"Can't I read in peace!"

"Come on," begged my sister. I knew that if I didn't say yes she would never give me peace.

"Okay, okay, okay, as long as you stop bugging me." I said with stress.

"See you tomorrow." my sister said. There was a evil smirk on her face.

The next day started stressfully. "Uhhhhhghhh! I'm dying in pain!" I tried to sound convincing to my sister. Maybe if I was sick, I wouldn't have to go.

"Come on, you promised" my sister said while dragging me out the door.

"OUCH! Let me go!"

I'm glad it's going to be a long car ride I moaned to myself. I would have done anything to not let the car ride end... but it did.

I stepped out of the car and took a look at the roller coasters. They were the absolute opposite of what I was expecting. I was expecting small and slow but they were big and fast. "Great, absolutely great," I said with sarcasm laced with anger.

As we awkwardly ran through the gates, I saw my friends, Jessica and Joyce coming off Superman, the roller coaster. Jessica's face was as white as snow. I asked them how was the ride.

"Absolutely wonderful," Jessica said as her eyes rolled back.

I could hear the sarcasm in her words.

Jessica pulled me over and said, "Joyce is the most horrible friend. She made me ride that chamber of horrors." Then Jessica said to Joyce "I almost died! It's is all your fault!"

I gulped, my mouth was as dry as a piece of grass that had not been watered for 20 days. As we lined up for Superman, I felt I was going to faint, weaker than a noodle. Fleeing out the gate and calling my mom to pick me up would have been my best decision but my sister yanked on me.

When it was our turn to ride Superman, I walked as slow as possible. I heard a few people snickering.

As I sat, they pulled a safety bar over me. I grabbed the closest person, which happened to be my sister. I asked "Are these really safe? Will they save my life if I fall? What will I do if I slip out of the safety bars?"

"Just be quiet and enjoy the ride," she said with great annoyance.

Then I had another vision. Did they put this bar on me because it's not safe? I tried to jump out. Too late!

My heart sounded like no ending thunder. I tried to close my eyes and calm my stress. No use! Nothing roamed in my brain but the word death....I heard in the distance a creaking sound. Could that mean that the roller coaster was about to start?

Before I could catch a breath, all of it was let out in a loud scream. My hands gripped the bars. My head was getting a shower in sweat. My heart practically burst from my chest. Nothing in my life at that moment mattered except the two words, roller coaster.

The roller coaster went fast, faster than a space shuttle. The endless spins and turns made feel like throwing up but that would be embarrassing so I held it in. Keeping the puke in felt like cleaning a toilet.

My head spun. I couldn't see. I thought that I would be dead before I could see the next sunrise.

The roller coaster slowed down a little bit. I peeked up. Right after... I wish I hadn't. Right in front of us was the biggest drop of the ride. People looked like ants, grass was impossible to see, even the clouds at this point looked possible to touch.

To me, it looked like we were even higher than the Statue of Liberty. My mind froze, I was paralyzed. Birds even looked scared to come this high above ground.

For once, I actually considered jumping off but I knew I'd die. I ended up staying, even though it was more painful.

"Here I go," I said with my voice shaking.

"Zoom," the roller coaster started.

"Ahhhh!" I heard my voice scream over all of the others.

"Hands up," my sister whispered.

"NEVER!" I yelled. The roller coaster went down down down.

My heart dropped. Suddenly the roller coaster stopped. Finally it was over.

When I got out of the cart, I kept questioning myself. Why did I say yes to my snobby, stupid sister. I told myself my sister was lucky, so lucky that I wouldn't kick her. I swore that not even a thousand dollars could get me on another roller coaster.

Maybe a million but not a thousand.

While I was running out of the gates I heard my sister say "Want to go again?" Not even a million bucks could get me to say yes.

~

The Mystery of the Skipping Stones

Emery E.

Henry and Anna were twins, both about five years of age. In the summer of 1986 they visited their grandma, Midge. One day they went out to play down by the lake at the foot of the small wood that surrounded Midge's home while Midge's housekeeper, Emily (though they called her Nanny) made lunch and Midge got a few minutes of shuteye.

When they got to the bottom of the hill Anna sat down on a flat rock about a foot off the ground. Henry however picked up a few skipping stones from the bank and threw the first stone. He watched the stone skip three skips then watched with amazement as it came skipping back! His jaws plummeted and when he glanced at Anna he saw that she was just as surprised as he was. He threw the next stone with a bit more force but it came back too. This time he threw the stone with all of his might but got the same results. Henry dropped all his stones, grabbed Anna's hand and ran back up to the house.

By the time that they reached the house it was lunchtime and Midge was at the table waiting for them. She immediately asked why they had taken so long for she had been worried. The children explained what happened and asked if she knew why it had happened. After a moment of thought she chuckled and said "You had some flying fish under your rocks and they wanted to get back to the shallower water because a predator was chasing them and it couldn't get them there". Anna and Henry laughed. They had a great rest of the summer and went back home in early autumn.

THE END

Not So Fun Now!

Emily R.

Jeffery was walking down the hallway laughing at people as always. Also this week was embarrassing. So here is how it all happened. Jeffery was at home in the kitchen with his dad. He had chocolate chip cookies with milk. He spilled his milk and left it there because he had no clue. His dad was going upstairs and walked on the milk and... WWWHHHOOSSHHH! Jeffery laughed so hard and dad yelled "THAT'S NOT FUNNY YOU ARE GROUNDED!" Jeffery giggled.

The next day Jeffery was playing baseball with his best friend max. When Max was supposed to catch the ball, the ball was already thrown and he was distracted and he turned around and the ball went right to his mouth! Jeffery was laughing as always. Max was angry and Jeffery said he was sorry.

When Jeffery was home he was watching TV with his older sister, Elizabeth. All of the sudden, Elizabeth's chair she was sitting on just fell to the floor but she was still sitting on it so she fell too. Jeffery was laughing so hard that his face turned red and he couldn't breathe. Elizabeth said with an angry voice "what are you laughing about! I just fell!" Jeffrey said that it was hilarious.

After that day Jeffery asked his mom if she can help him with his homework. She said yes. When he asked what was 24 + 60 and his mom knew the correct answer but she made a mistake and said it was 83. But Jeffrey knew that it was 84 so he laughed at her. His mom said "I knew what the answer was so no laughing." Jeffery didn't believe her.

Jeffery was licking ice cream and everyone was there. Then he licked it again and the ice cream scoop fell into his pants and everyone started to laugh except Jeffery. He yelled "THAT'S NOT FUNNY!" Everyone said well it wasn't funny what happened to us either. Dad said "I know how it feels," Jeffery said with a sorry voice "I am very sorry at everyone." Then everyone did a group hug.

KONY 2012
and The Invisible Children

Gabi S.

Once upon a time there was an evil man named Joseph Kony.

He took kids from their beds, homes, and parents. Not just a few. Over 30,000 children. He abducted and abused them. He gave them guns and made them child slaves. Then they had no choice over what they did next. They were forced to kill their own parents, and possibly other people too.

But this is no fairy tale. This is happening in Uganda RIGHT NOW. Kids that are in hiding are being slammed into crummy spaces, and sleeping 2 inches apart or less. These are the invisible children. And we have to help them.

For the past 30 years Kony has been doing this. He is not doing it for a specific reason, or for war, but to stay in power. Almost no one knew who he was when he started. Now millions of people know who he is. You might think he would be captured if millions of people know who he is. But millions are not enough. Everyone has to know before he can be overpowered.

But now, more and more people are making Joseph Kony famous. That is good for us. Some of the world's most famous people are helping spread the news about Kony. Justin Bieber spread it online. All this publicity is bad for Kony and good for us. And along with Justin Bieber are Rihanna and Oprah. Kony must be known. The best way to understand how Kony's actions, watch KONY 2012 on you-tube. Kony has to be stopped. U.S soldiers were send into Uganda a while ago. Disastrously, he found out and changed his tactics. We are getting closer, but the U.S. might give up and leave it to Uganda. The only way to let him know that we are coming is to make he knows he has been discovered. He isn't on the Police Most Wanted List. He isn't even on America's Most Wanted List. He is on Earth's Most Wanted List.

~

Chester, the Loud Mouse

Hannah L.

Chester loved to talk, talk and talk. He talked when eating, talked when in the bathroom, and even talked in his sleep! He also talked very loud. When he is whispering, it sounds like human speaking. When he is talking, it sounds like a human shout, and when he shouts, it sounds 10 times louder than a human shout.

One day, Chester's village, Cheeseville, ran out of cheese for the mice, Chester was invited to go hunting for cheese in the Brisky's pantry. The mice that were going were Chester's friends. Everyday they practiced their hunting skills. But the mice had to watch out for Snipper, aka the Popkin Beast. Snipper was the cat of sharp eared Mr. Brisky and deaf eared Mrs. Brisky. Since Mr. Brisky was out of town, the mice didn't need to worry about him; Mrs. Brisky would never be able to hear Chester.

As night came, Chester and his friend shuck out. As they headed towards the pantry, they saw Snipper guarding the door as usual. At that moment, Chester screamed, "Holy Cheese!" Snipper woke up and jumped towards them. Oh, oh, Snipper was attacking! One of Chester's friend climbed on Snipper's back and said, "Giddy Up!" Then he fell down and Snipper hissed at him. Suddenly, Chester had an idea. He and his friends understood sign language. Chester held up one paw because it meant, "Go!" so he used the hand signals to get away from Snipper and steal the cheese.

When Chester and his friends got back, everyone cheered "Hooray!" From then on, every mouse had cheese. They always used Chester's hand signals when hunting for cheese, even though Chester was the loudest mouse in Cheeseville.

~

Mike and the Lost Bike

Healey K.

I woke up, brushed my teeth, ate breakfast, and got dressed. It was very quiet while I did my morning routine in my abandoned house.

I stepped into the desolate garage to grab my bike to ride to Stevenson High School, when I noticed my bike was not in the garage. The garage smelled of rotting food while I searched for my bike. It was as dark and damp as a jail cell. I couldn't find it in the stinky, dark, damp and quiet garage.

I searched all over the empty, lonely and quiet house. I peeked through the screen door on the porch because I sometimes come through the front door when I get home from school. I checked the patio also through the screen door because I sometimes leave my bike on the patio. I even checked the storage room because my mom puts anything she finds in there.

I looked frantically. It was so quiet, I could hear my own heartbeat. I thought, oh, how I wish I had my bike. I figured I'd just have to walk to school.

I started walking in the chilly November air. I saw my neighbor and waved to him.

He waved back and said, "Have fun at school, Mike!" to me.

I smelled something, maybe burnt wood. As I was walking I noticed the clouds. They were dark and big, very, very big. I thought to myself I would be at school right now if I had my bike.

All of a sudden, white stuff started to fall out of the sky. At first I thought, oh, it's nothing. Then it started to come down faster and faster like a blizzard. I didn't care if everybody heard me because I was horrified. So I shouted at the top of my lungs, "SNOW!"

I started to run. My legs moved as fast as they could. I could've biked to school faster than running. My heart was pounding. My heart went, b-boom, b-boom. I was getting really hot. Until, SCHOOL!

I sat down in my wet and white clothes at the only empty desk left in science class. Someone told me the teacher just announced that Spike was sick with pneumonia. He wouldn't be back for about a week.

I cried to myself quietly, "Awwwwww." I couldn't believe Spike was sick; he was my only friend. Nobody was talking to me. I probably would have felt better if I had my bike. I was very lonely and blue.

The day finally came to an early end at 1:00 p.m. I looked at the calendar and saw it was Friday. "Yikes!" Tomorrow is the weekend and I don't have my bike. How am will I get to soccer practice and visit my grandma.

I started packing my backpack full with books as fast as I could so I could start looking for my bike early. I checked the school inside and out. Then I remembered!

It was raining the day before today, and my mom picked me up from school. I must have left my bike on the bike rack. I dashed to the bike rack, and there it was! I found it! I found my bike!

I biked home as fast as I could just to find my mom scowling. I knew my mom was mad at me for being late for a special sushi lunch with her. Luckily, she didn't know about the missing bike.

~

"Terrify Your Teacher"

Isabelle J.

To terrify your teacher
You have to be a spy
To see what makes her scream
By watching with one eye.
While she's teaching math
Sword-fight with the rulers
Write equations on the walls
And yell loudly like preschoolers.
While he's teaching gym
Don't listen to the rules
Hog the climbing rope
And act like crazy fools.
During art enrichment
Color on the walls
Step on all the paints
And scream up and down the halls.
Pretend that you are interested
In your science class
Make loud, quirky noises
And often let out gas.
In the cafeteria
Make a real big mess
Dump the ravioli
On the teacher's dress.
While he is teaching music
Start singing way off key
Squeak with your recorder
And start laughing with much glee.
But to really terrify him
Be polite and kind
Then he'll really wonder
What's going on in that devilish mind?

Hachi, the Brave

Jessica W.

"Hachi fetch!" I cried.

Hachi sprinted as fast as lightning across the backyard and leapt up catching the blue and white whirling Frisbee.

Hachi and I were enjoying a breezy fall day outside playing Frisbee. He darted back to me panting deeply, his ears perky, his eyes happy and his golden-brown fur blowing with the wind.

Hachi nudged my elbow. He seemed to enjoy the thrill of running freely in the wind. Leaping up and down seemed to make him feel a soaring sensation like he was above the clouds.

As I threw the Frisbee again, Hachi dashed after it. Unexpectedly a draft of wind carried it into a tree. I darted and leapt up, trying to grab the Frisbee, but fell to the ground.

When I gazed up, the Frisbee was stuck in the highest tree branch. No problem I thought, all I had to do was climb up the tree, go on the branch, seize the Frisbee and then descend.

"Hachi sit," I commanded him. Then I said my voice firm, "Now stay until I get down."

Hachi barked in protest, his face drooping slightly but then rolled around on his back in reluctant agreement. I rubbed his white fluffy belly.

Then I clambered up the tree. The tree swayed a little with the wind. I climbed up branch-by-branch grabbing onto any branch within my reach that would support me.

When I got to the Frisbee I felt a surge of relief flow through me. But when I peered down, I became frightened.

Oh darn it!!! I forgot I was scared of heights. Though I wanted to look down to check on Hachi, I couldn't get my muscles to do it. Fear clung to me like a predator clinging to its prey.

I climbed further down the branch and grabbed the Frisbee.

Yipee!!!! I thought, now I can proceed down to Hachi, I couldn't have been more wrong.

Just before I left the branch, it creaked. For a moment I heard only the creaking of the branch and the wind. Every bird chirping, leaves rustling, sounded like the creaking and cracking of the branch. For a moment I actually considered jumping off the branch, but I knew I would get an injury from the sharp branches and twigs below me and I would tumble down to the ground bruised and scratched.

I looked down at Hachi on the ground that seemed miles below. He watched me curiously his head tilted to its side. Though I didn't know what he was thinking I knew he was wondering why I was hanging from the branch, my face purple.

Suddenly, the branch gave another sharp lurching jab with only about half a centimeter left connected to the tree. I was 0 inches from screaming. "HHHHHEEEELLLLPPPP!!!!!" I cried.

Hachi was all ears, he barked as loud as a siren. My parents and neighbors couldn't hear me, and I was definitely not prepared to die.

OOOOOOOOOOWWWWWWWWW!!!!! My arms couldn't hold the

branch any longer; I took a sharp breath. I felt as if I couldn't have one thing in my grasp any longer.

Suddenly, the branch broke, I plunged down right out of the tree. I dropped and dropped through twigs and branches. I received a variety of scratches and bumps until I landed on something, a wooden board, a stone, a tree trunk, or maybe Hachi?

My mind started to twitch uncomfortably and I somehow drifted off to sleep. When I woke up I was in a daze and thought why was I here? Feeling a soft patch of fur next to my ear, I felt along to touch Hachi.

Then I remembered, something had caught me and broke my fall. What was it? Even though my leg was injured, as it had been twisted in tangled branches.... it should have been hurt worse falling from that height. I got up writhing with pain to find my mom, but my leg's pain felt unbearable so I dropped to the ground.

When I looked over at Hachi, he lay on his side, with sad eyes, whimpering in pain. I screamed realizing it was Hachi that caught me.

"MOM! HELP! PLEASE! I THINK I BROKE MY LEFT LEG AND HACHI IS HURT BADLY!" I stood up again to walk writhing with pain. I had to help Hachi. But I couldn't stand the pressure on my leg.

Out of nowhere, my mother appeared. It all came out of me in a rush. I told my mom about failing to catch the Frisbee, falling from the tree, Hachi saving me, and finally the pain in my leg. But most importantly I said, "We've got to take Hachi to the animal hospital."

She smiled and said, "I'm glad you're safe, Jessica."

I returned her smile and replied, "Thanks, but remember...," I looked at my leg puffed up swollen and as green as grass.

My mom uncertainly said, "Just in case, I think you need to go to the hospital." I reluctantly nodded in agreement.... but I insisted that Hachi go first.

~

Case of the Missing Trophies

Joyce B.

"Rachel, don't do that, you might get in trouble," I yelled at my risky friend. It was March 30th. I walked down the entrance hall of Daniel Wright Junior High School on my way to the cafeteria.

Out of the corner of my eye, I saw a sign near the trophy case. It read "Whoever finds the criminal who stole the trophy will get rewarded."

Puzzled, I looked at the case. It was missing a trophy. I asked Rachel if she wanted to help, but she wasn't interested in helping me find the missing trophy....until I mentioned we would get rewarded.

Rachel immediately began to bang on the case hoping it would open so she could find some clues, but it was no use. The case had a key and the only person that had it was the principal. I rushed to the principal's office and got the key. Rachel was making a scene, of course. I was used to her behavior.

When I opened the case, I began searching for evidence. I gazed into the case for a while. Then a brightly colored piece of paper caught my eye. It was sticking out from under a trophy. It read: "If you find this note, it is your first step. Check everywhere for another clue. I am probably in the school."

What??? I read the note over and over again but I couldn't figure it out. I thought whoever this so-called burglar was, he was just playing games or he wouldn't have left the note.

After lunch I rushed down to the principal's office because if this criminal stole the trophies, he probably stole something from the principal's office too. I scanned the office up and down, but I couldn't find anything missing. Rachel, of course, was opening cabinets and making a mess. I wasn't surprised, she was always like this.

I kept searching, then out of the corner of my eye I saw a note in between two cabinets. It said: "If you found my first note then you're on the right track, I am not who you think I am. I see you all the time."

What does he mean... he sees me all the time. The only ones who can see me are my classmates and all of the school staff. Since there weren't any rhymes or patterns, the burglar was probably planning something big. I was really curious now. I needed some ideas.

Rachel suggested we should wait after school and jump out when he comes because the criminal just stole one trophy and might steal more. We would be able to catch him red handed.

Before she could do something dangerous, I said we should just put a video camera in the trophy case and check it in the morning. She hated that idea because we didn't break into the school and capture someone, but she agreed.

In the morning, I rushed to the case with Rachel trailing behind me and checked our video camera. I was eager to know who stole the trophies. When I rolled the video clip, I saw the principal sneakily walking down the hall looking left and right for anyone around. Then he opened the cabinet, took the trophy and then took it back to his office. He also slipped a note under the last trophy. He checked to see if the other notes I found were there, then he smiled and walked away.

After I saw the video, I was outraged, as mad as a tricked gorilla. Why in the world would the principal steal his own school trophies, make everyone uncomfortable, and make me so worried I couldn't sleep.

I snatched the note almost knocking down the trophy. It read "If you find this note then you must have found the others. You have to find me today or you will never succeed. Good luck."

Huh? What was so special about Friday, April 1st.

Madly I marched down to the principal's office with Rachel trailing behind me and showed him the clip. He smiled and muttered "smart kids." He gave us certificates and congratulated us.

I frowned, puzzled, and asked him why he pretended to be a robber and "steal" the trophies.

Our crazy principal chortled and boomed, "APRIL FOOL'S".

I didn't know what to do laugh or get mad!

Spring

Kavya K.

It is a wonderful time of the year
The sun stays out longer
Flowers are in bloom
Animals are out from hibernation
Children play outside
Birds are singing
And dandelions fly everywhere
Spring is the season which brings color and fun.

~

When I Do This, I Feel That

Konoka Y.

When I step outside the door,
I feel that feeling it is warm.
When I eat my snack first,
I feel that feeling I get sick.
When I go to school late,
I feel that feeling I am pain.
When I sleep very early,
I get that feeling I'm so awake.
When my mom says nice things,
I feel that feeling I'm awesome.
When I think of a lot of things,
I get that feeling every time.

~

Reversing Roles

Lexie B.

You know how most fantasies have, "Once upon a time...", and, "They lived happily ever after."? How they have princes saving princesses? This story isn't like that. This time, we're reversing roles.

In a small kingdom, there lived a very beautiful princess. The thing is, she wasn't like most princesses. Because she was an only child, and her mother died when she was born, she was like the son her father never had. She was the best hunter, the best fighter, and even the best jouster. She always knew her consequences, whether they were good or bad.

Now (as the story always goes), there was a deadline for her to get married. Princes from all over came to court her. Many of them are handsome but were on the lower end of the intelligence scale. She refused all of the suitors.

Because she wanted to get away from having to marry, she ran away with her sword and bow, along with her favorite hound. She went into the woods and heard yelling and a large crash.

She ran into a large clearing and saw a golden dragon. In its claws there was a young prince. He was the one that was yelling.

The princess leaped into action. She unsheathed her sword and bow and confronted the dragon. She slashed its legs and made contact. It roared and fell down with an enormous crash. She slaughtered it and freed the prince from the dead dragon's talons.

He told her that he had been on his way to court the nearby princess when the beast grabbed him. Several minutes later, she had come running up to defeat the dragon. He thanked her for saving his life, and then he asked who she was. In reply, she told him that she was the princess. In shock, he asked her where she had learned to fight so well. Of course, she told him she had learned from her father.

So, when she showed up at home, she told her father about whom she met in the forest. Now, like in every other fantasy, they got married the next day, and instead of living happily ever after, they lived better than that. They lived joyfully ever after.

The End

Trouble

Lindsey G.

My life could have been ruined.

This is how it all started. But first let me introduce myself, my name is Ashley, I'm 11 so things can get tough.

So let's begin.

It all started on a Monday, no a Wednesday, no. Okay just forget it. It was a weekday, and I was walking down the hall I tripped on a mean bully named: JOE.

Yes you might have heard the things about him and they are true. So when I tripped he tripped too. It was not my fault he tripped. So at the very moment the bell rang. I was so scared, but I got even more scared when I heard him walk to class because I heard him say, "I will get my revenge".

The next day I got even more scared because it was Friday the 13th.

At lunch he had chicken nuggets and ketchup and I had macaroni and cheese. I guess someone pushed me because I spilled my macaroni all over him.

Then when no one was looking he pushed himself on the ground to make it look I pushed him. Then when no one was looking again he took his ketchup and put it under his nose to make it look like I punched him.

Then someone told the teacher and I had to go to her office on Monday at lunch.

Over the weekend I told my mom what happened and she said not to worry but how can you tell someone that, when they are already worried that just made me more worried.

On Monday Joe told me if I told the teacher what really happened he would make it so I would not be able to go to school any more. Creepy right?

So I told the teacher that it was my entire fault.

The teacher asked if she could talk to me private

This is what she said “what has gotten into you, you are a very good student” It is all Joe, I said. She said I need prove. I started to think, okay I got it, look at the security cameras.

She saw and said help me think of a punishment. I know he has to eat and learn with you for the rest of the year.

Then she said, Joe come in here. And it was very weird because he said he heard and then he screamed NOOOOOOOOOOOOOOOOOOO OOOOOOOOOO.

That is how I dealt with that bully.

THE END

A Rainy Ride

Madeleine O.

It's rainy today.
The bus slides on the slick streets.
The bus is quiet.
People play their games
On I-Pods and D.S.'s.
The world's quiet here.
As we reach our school,
Puddles of water go splash.
Thunder crackles loud.

~

The Secret Stone

Matthew B.

Narrator: Once upon a time there was a tornado in Texas two explorers were in a car and they were going to Minnesota. Then the tornado hit their car then their car bounced somewhere far away.

Bob and John: Ahhhhhhhhhhhhhhhhhhh!!!!!!!!!!!!!!

John: Glad that's done.

Bob: Where are we?!

John: I do not know!

Bob: Look at that cave! Let's go inside it.

John: Here we are.

Witch: How dare you come in my fancy house/cave.

Bob: Who are you!

Witch: I am a witch. I live here.

John: How can you live here?

Bob: What do you eat?

Witch: STOP! Get out! But if you want to stay you have to find a stone if you get the stone you can stay and ask as many questions you want.

John: How much time?

Witch: Two days.

Bob: What are you going to do with the stone?

John: Then why do you want the stone?

Witch: It does not matter! If you do not get it in two days I will put a curse on both of you. Your time starts now!

John: Let's go!

Bob: Let's do this.

Narrator: So John and Bob went out on their amazing journey.

John: Which way should we go first?

Bob: Let's go that way!

John: But, if that way does not work we are going back, okay?

Narrator: So the two men had an amazing guess because they got in the right way!

Bob: Which way now?

John: How many places to go in? There is about 8 ways to go. Let's go in the one that was to the right.

Bob: Good thinking!

Narrator: It has been 1 day. The story is in the middle of the story. Another witch is going for it, too.

John: Let's use our speedy fast power.

Narrator: The witch grabbed it.

Bob: Let's grab it.

Narrator: They grabbed it.

John: I have to do something. Good thing I have a translator!

In a single flash they went back to the cave.

All: We got it!!!!!!!!!!!!!!!!!!!!!!!!!!!!!!!!

The End

Tommy the Cat

Max B.

Once upon a time there was a cat named Tommy. Tommy had no friends at all. But one day his mom said, "Why don't you go outside and make some friends?" So he did. He went over to the park. And said does anyone want to be my friend? Only one cat said yes. A cat named Billy. Billy said can you help me with something? Sure said Tommy. There's a bully. What!!!!!!!!! Said Tommy. You're so nice how could you be bullied? Tommy said, "Let's go stop the bully." "But wait a minute but how are we going to find this guy?"

Billy said, "I know where he hangs out."

Well then tell me. Ok, He hangs out at the park. Let's go on an adventure to the park! So they went to the park. When they got there the bully said, "Hi, Billy you got the money?" Tommy said, "He doesn't need to give you any money." Well I'm bigger and older than both of you. So if Billy doesn't give me money he gets hurt. "Well, is there a reason for that buddy?" said Tommy No, he said. Then why are you doing it? I want to. Time out said Billy. You said that it was because you had to give somebody the money. Well my advice to you is to go talk to that guy. The bully said, "Oky doke see ya." The two friends went with the bully. But when they got there, the guy was Billy's dad. Billy is so surprised, he says "Dad, What!" and the bully's dad says "surprise, Happy Birthday!"

And they all lived happily ever after.

~

Bella's Story

Michelle V.

Bella did not think she was pretty. Actually, she thought she was ugly. She had curly red hair, a dusting of freckles and was very, very clumsy. She was the clumsiest girl in her orphanage. She was also the youngest. Both of these were big disadvantages. The whole orphanage taunted her because she had red hair. Even Miss Minchin, the teacher picked on her whenever she could. Suddenly, her oldest sister, Rachel interrupted her thoughts. "Bella!" Rachel called. "Come here this instant!" What does she want now? Bella thought. "What is the meaning of this?" asked Rachel, holding up a pillowcase that looked heavy. "What is the meaning of what?" Bella said. "You put rocks into this pillowcase!" Rachel said. "No breakfast for you!" "That isn't not fair!" bellowed Bella, and then she ran to her room. A few minutes later, her best friend Alexis came into her room. Alexis was very pretty with wavy brown hair and dark blue eyes. "Remember about our expedition?" asked Alexis. "Yes, let's review" Bella said. "First, we get to the beach. Then, we find The House of Shadows with the fortune teller lady that is rumored to live there. Lastly, we find out what our fortune is. It's simple." How are we going to pay for it?" asked Alexis. "We have enough money combined," answered Bella. "Alright. When should we put our plan into action?" asked Alexis. "How about during lunch break?" said Bella. "Sure." replied Alexis. But what the girls did not know was that Bella's younger brother, Danny was eavesdropping on them and heard their plan. He immediately went to tell his brothers and sisters about it. Rachel, Ariella, Jake and Ben were all sitting on the floor, talking. Danny sat down and told them about what he had heard. When he was finished, everyone was shocked, "How dare they?" Ariella blurted out. "Should we tell Miss Minchin?" asked Ben. "No, not this time. Maybe we can get our own fortune too. Okay. Here's the plan," said Rachel. As they discussed how they were going to intrude Bella and Alexis's expedition, the two girls quietly reviewed their plan again and again. When the bell finally rang the girls slipped out of Bella's room. They got out of the room and downstairs okay but when they got to the door, they were stopped by all of Bella's sisters and brothers. "We want to know our fortune too." Danny said. "How did you know?" exclaimed Alexis. "Alright. I was eavesdropping. Danny admitted. "Now with that said let's get a fortune!" said Bella. They then left the orphanage and went outside. Even though it was late April, it was still cold outside. "All right," Bella said. "The beach is about a mile away from here. If we run, we will make it back by lunch time." So they all ran silently and only stopped when they got to the beach. When they looked around they realized they had no clue where to go. "What are we going to do?" cried Alexis. "Oh, Alexis, Alexis, always the doubtful one! I brought a map!" exclaimed Bella. And following the map, they all found the House of Shadows. Ben knocked on the door and a sleepy voice answered. "Come in". The voice said. They came in and paid the money. "We want to know our future," said Danny. "Danny, don't be so rude," said Rachel. "Your future looks good, bright, and happy. Someone will claim you, all of you. But Bella, yours is even better, you're special." With that they left and returned to the orphanage. A year passed. Then two. Everything was normal. Bella occasionally got into trouble. Then, on a cold winter day around noon, an older man and his wife came and told Miss Minchin that they always wanted to have kids but were never able to have any. They wanted three girls and three boys that were all related. Miss Minchin immediately led him to Bella's room, where Bella was drawing on a scrap piece of paper, the boys were playing cards and Rachel and Arielle were talking. The whole room silenced when Miss Minchin and the man and his wife came in. "Yes." The man said. "We would like them." He introduced himself and his wife as Mr. and Mrs. Williamson. So Bella and her siblings were to pack their things. They didn't have a lot, so it didn't take long. In less than ten minutes they were on their way to the couple's house. When they arrived, they were all very tired. Their house didn't look very different from a castle. They all got their own rooms and Mr and Mrs. Willliamson were very kind to them. They gave them huge meals, big comfy beds, a beautiful room, and Bella could visit Alexis whenever she liked. The kids were always happy...

Fifteen Years Later

Bella and Danny were waiting in a restaurant for Alexis, Ben, Jake, Ariella, and Rachel. They had arranged a reunion since they hadn't seen each other for a long time. At that very moment, Alexis rushed in through the door. "Bella!" said Alexis. The two girls hugged and hugged each other. The girls talked about their lives and then, one by one, Ben, Jake, Ariella, and Rachel came. They all had a big dinner and promised to do it every few years. And, well I guess you could say everyone lived happily ever after.

The End

Four Seasons

Nora B.

PART ONE: SPRING

When I wake up today,
the sun streaming through the open windows,
licking my face and begging me to come outside,
I swing myself out of my cozy bead in a heartbeat,
throwing on my clothes and stepping into my boots,
not bothering to make my bed or eat breakfast.
Without thinking or caring about anything else,
my boots whizzing through the mildewy grass,
I dance through the puddles of last night's rain,
and listen to the quiet, peaceful humming,
of the calming atmosphere around me.
This dreamlike world around me is all mine,
as I lay down on the grass, without a care in the world,
and close my eyes without realizing so,
the ticklish texture of millions of blades of grass,
wrapping me like a blanket,
and the scent of floral fragrance engaging me,
as I too easily drift off to sleep.

PART TWO: SUMMER

Jumping out of my bed,
at the first sight of golden sunshine,
I pull up the delicate straps of my silky bathing suit,
running down the stairs and out the door,
and after quickly grabbing a bite to eat,
I race all the way down the road,
to meet the still aqua waters of the glittering pool.
I swiftly jump out of the hot sticky air,
into the cool calmness of the water,
and listen to the faraway laughter of my friends,
too dreamy to pay attention,
to the meaning of the words they spoke.
As I step out of my wonderland,
I feel the warm air rejoice around me,
as I gulp down ice cold lemonade,
laughing along with my friends,
in wordless understanding.
After hours of playing in the sun,
I run back down the road,
dripping wet and feeling my bare feet burn,
on the scorching hot blacktop,
just barely able to make it home,
.....and in time for dinner.

PART 3: AUTUMN

Before you would think to go outside,
I always find myself out there in early morning,
smelling in the fresh autumn cinnamon scented air,
and I sit up in my tree house to relax,
and to watch as delicate leaves flutter to the ground,
mixing the grass with colors of red, gold, and even purple.
I grab my bike and jump on,
pumping the pedals,
as I listen to the birds create their own music,
a harmonic symphony,
as they migrate south,
to get away from the bitter cold.
I think and breath this colder weather,
as I jump into an enormous pile of multicolored leaves,
and feel the padded earth beneath me,
I stare as the day turns to midday, then afternoon.........
and finally nightfall.
Crisp night air circles around me,
as the last beam of sunlight fades away into the heavens,
leaving a night filled with stars and the night's cool breeze,
and I sleepily pull myself inside
the welcoming doors of my house.

PART FOUR: WINTER

I look out through the white tinted window,
watching as fragile flakes of crystal float down,
layering into piles of freshly fallen snow,
as I pull on my gear and leap into the wintery blizzard.
I dance in my world of pure bliss,
the cold air whipping around me in a frenzy,
as I lay down on the snow,
letting the frozen ice chill my face,
the peaceful calmness engulfing me.
The quiet, woody atmosphere surrounding me,
my numb fingertips brushing the icy cold crystals,
as I close my eyes,
and puff out soft, cool air,
cold down to the bone,
and frozen just the same.
the sky rapidly turning dark right before my eyes,
the sun rushing downward,
and being replaced by a million twinkling bulbs of light,
my frazzled brain slowing down,
as I slump into my bed,
with my boots still on,
as I very quickly lose consciousness,
and drift to sleep.

Oceans of Wonder

Ojasvi S.

Oceans, oh oceans, of wonder,
I wonder what lies beneath the ocean water!
With so much life under the surface,
I wish I could see the different zones.

~

The Euphotic zone full of flying fish, eel, manta rays and many wonders

Mesopelagic zone full of scary sharks, and crustacean, lantern fish?, and a whole lot more

As, the Bathypelagic zone contains many whales, hatchet fish and so much more

Finally, the Abyssal zone, has deep sea fish, tube worms and so many more wonders.

~

The Pacific is the Supreme Ruler of the oceans as it's 63.8 million square miles in total area

The Atlantic is the 2nd biggest ocean at 41.1 million square miles. Did you know that it is interconnected to all the different oceans?

Who rules next?

Is it the Southern or the Indian Ocean???

It is the Indian Ocean at 28.4 million square miles

Then we have the Southern ocean, only identified in the spring of 2000, at 7.9 million square miles

Finally, we find the Artic, at 5.6 million square miles.

And that's the ocean wonders of the world!

(That's been discovered so far!)

~

Unicorns Are Scary Things

Olivia L.

Unicorns are scary things
I hate those horns with golden rings
Silky fur causes me to scream
They gallop through my scariest dreams
Some may think they are great as pets
The thought of that makes me sweat
Fairy tales say they are sweet
I bet these horses would enjoy me as a treat
All my life I've waited for
Them to come knocking at my door
Claiming they are quite nice
They'll eat me up with carrots and rice
Those tails could easily act as rope
Strangling away my very last hope
Don't even ask me about their neighs
They're battle calls in many ways
They say that I'm scared of something strange
But I know their thoughts will definitely change
When they are sitting at home alone
And a unicorn starts to gnaw on their bones
What did you say?
Is that something I hear?
Why are you giggling? Why do you laugh?
What do you mean I've been scared of something
fake for a year and a half?

~

A Day with Native Americans

Pallavi P.

I blinked the sleepiness out of my eyes as I slowly stretched. "Where am I?" I wondered. My question was answered by a lady that was cleaning. "We found you and your whole neighborhood surrounded by smoking pieces of metal. What was that?" "Yeah, that was our time machine. It was built by my father, Billy Jones III. He is a famous inventor. He invented the solar powered car, solar powered lawnmower and some other stuff. I bet that you didn't understand a single word that I said. This is all stuff of the future. We were going to the prehistoric times, then to the Roman times. I know this probably doesn't make sense to you." I replied. "You're right. It doesn't. By the way, you are inside my tepee. I am Sitting Sheep of the Sioux tribe. My father, Dakota, is the chief of this tribe," she replied. As I surveyed the tepee, I saw that the inside was filled with feathers, painted buffalo, and spears. There was a warm fire in the middle. I saw that I was sleeping on a big buffalo hide, probably from an adult buffalo.

I thought about what my teacher had told us when we were learning about the Sioux in class. They lived in the Black Hills of South Dakota. They were originally called Nadouessioux. The Sioux lived in tepees made from buffalo hides. They ate fruit, berries, nuts, roots, and buffalo. Sioux wore clothes made from animals they hunted. The girls played with handmade dolls. The men were excellent warriors. The women cooked, cleaned, and made clothes while the boys practiced hunting. Sitting Sheep prodded me, and I came back to the present.

Sitting Sheep offered me some pemmican for breakfast. Pemmican is crushed up meat, berries, fruit, and nuts with melted buffalo fat poured over the mixture. The mixture was gooey like peanut butter, salty like cashews, and warm. It was pretty good! I took off my old clothes and slipped into a deerskin dress decorated with seashells, and some buffalo hide moccasins that Sitting Sheep had offered me. "Where is everyone?" I asked. "Explore the village. You will find them," Sitting Sheep said.

As I came out of the tepee to explore the indigenous village, I found my mother helping some Sioux women with their chores. "Madison!" my mom called me. I walked towards her and started helping the women put elk teeth on the dress they were making. "Where did you get the teeth?" I asked. "They came from an elk that Crazy Horse killed." "Cool!" This dress is a gift for Sitting Sheep. As I looked around, I saw smoke rising from the other tepees, which could only mean one thing, people were cooking. I also saw men coming back from their long hunt, loaded with buffalo. Just then Sitting Sheep came through and said, "Come along! Today is Crazy Horse's birthday!" Crazy Horse was the best warrior in the tribe and also the strongest. At the festival, we sang and danced. I found my friends Liz, Emma, and Cindy. They were wearing the same clothes as me! A little girl taught us how to make dolls. After we made the dolls, we showed them to our mothers and played with them. It was getting dark, so some men lit torches and placed them around us. They were made from buffalo fat and sticks. The torches shined brighter than the brightest star in the pitch black night.

At the festival, we all realized that we were starving, since we skipped lunch. For dinner we had wild turkey, fish, and berries. After dinner I went to Sitting Sheep's tepee and fell asleep. My mom woke me up in the middle of the night. "We repaired the time machine! Let's go!" she whispered. We crept out of the tepee and into the time machine. ZOOM! Suddenly we were in the prehistoric time. That's another story.

~

Opening Eyes

Philip R.

Her eyes shot open, and she sat up with a million questions running through her head. Where was she?

She wandered around. She had so many questions she thought her head would blow up. But then a word popped into his her head, "Anna Belle"...

After walking down the road for a while, she saw a building that looked like a school. She finally reached the building, and she saw that it WAS a school. No one was on the playground, and it looked deserted. But she did notice how clean it was. So she walked over to the door and pulled on the handle; the door swung open revealing a long hallway.

She started down the hall and saw that some of the lockers were open and containing items. She could now tell that the school was not deserted. Suddenly she heard a voice, it was faint but she knew she heard it. She kept on walking, and at the end of the hallway she found the root of the sound. She turned and found a sign that read "Principal's Office". She put her ear to the door and heard a man say "Yeah a student disappeared a while ago. I couldn't blame her. If my parents died I would run from the orphanage. Yeah that's her, "Elizabeth". That word shot into her head and she realized that it was her name.

Elizabeth ran down the hall and out the door. It was dark and she knew she would need to find shelter.

Elizabeth searched around but didn't find any place to stay. She decided to go back into the school and find somewhere to sleep, but she didn't want to go in until the man was out.

While Elizabeth was thinking, she heard a door opening and then the sound of a motor starting up. Then there was silence as the car drove away. She dashed through the school doors that were carelessly left open. She found the teacher's lounge where a soft couch was waiting for her and she fell asleep.

The Great Match

Praneet R.

Hi, I am the son of a king. Our castle is in Cairo, Egypt and we live close to a mysterious pyramid. Are you a person travels a lot? I am one of those people. I have been to so many places that the number is uncountable (I was actually born in China!).

Recently, my mind has been kind of going crazy. I have been hearing a lot of whispering about magic, power, wands and so much more. I hear words like the five deadly days and the House. Aren't you heartbroken when someone in your family passes out? That was exactly what had happened on Christmas. Here is the whole story. We, my mom, dad, and my grandpa whose name is Cantabala and my uncle all went to a museum. It was the Egyptian Rock Exploring Museum. We walked through the entrance and went to the section that had rocks from the 2000 B.C. time frame. One rock in particular grabbed my interest. It was large rock named Romennakl stone. Meanwhile, in the distance I saw my uncle touching the rock in and the rock started glowing with red hieroglyphics surrounding it. The rock started to tremble and shake, finally it exploded. Then uncle whispered a few words and another rock started to form and it grumbled "Die or surrender" with that, after a long minute of silence a fight broke out. As soon as I knew it uncle was lying on the ground, and he disappeared.

TEN YEARS LATER

To this day I still have that vivid memory in the back of my mind. I am now nineteen years old. I still live with my mom, dad, and wise old grandpa, Cantabala.

I was sitting on my couch with a room full of silence. I asked why my uncle played with the Romennakl Stone. Grandpa replied that "There is a fearsome man named Romennakl. Romennakl is bad. We tried to destroy him. His life was stuck into that stone. We tried to change the stone's name to Maltoc, the good god. I told uncle to destroy the stone and create a new stone, but he... " Grandpa broke out crying. It was my mistake to ask uncle to take that responsibility. "It is not your fault" I said. "You can't do anything about it" I tried to comfort him. He didn't reply.

Suddenly, I heard a BIG BOOM!!! It was from upstairs. I dashed out of the room, and ran upstairs as fast as lightening and stumbled into my parent's room followed by Grandpa. I gasped what a dreadful sight, there I saw the real live Romennakl fighting my parents. Suddenly my parents fell to the ground soaked of blood and vanished into the thin air. It was my turn, I scrambled to get my sword slashed it against Romennakl and after a those horrible ten minutes a cave appeared. Romennakl stepped in and as soon as I knew it he went away. Romennakl disappeared. I guessed that the thing was a magical, invisible move. Grandpa explained it was called a Shubu in our Egyptian language.

Did you know in fifteen days, it is going to be Christmas and my birthday! The fifteen days zoomed by and as soon as I knew it, my birthday came and I got a bundle of presents. My favorite gifts were nine silky lights and shiny blue wands with a smooth and soft texture. I also got a mini tiger. From my schema, I know that a tiger is an animal for our culture. We used tiger in Mlandv kingdom. I also got a necklace that had a drawing of the first ruler of the successful Mlandv kingdom. Inside one of the bag and there was a soft leathery piece of paper and it had a carving that looked very pretty. That carved soft paper is symbol future Egyptian kings. My grandpa said that if I blow the paper, I will become the future king. I decided to wait on that one. I pulled out some more of papers from the bag; each one had a different figure on it. One figure represented having a great power.

The next day morning, when I opened my sensitive eyes, my grandpa picked me up in a rush and tossed me into the car. I bounced into the car with a huge thud. After a few minutes, when we were on the road Grandpa told me we were going to Jerusalem, Israel. I haven't been there for ages and ages. As soon as I knew we were cruising to Israel with ultrasonic speed. My Grandpa told me about my parents and Romennakl were fighting. My parents actually didn't die.

My parents just turned invisible and went to Israel. Sure enough, like how grandpa had said, when we landed we had company, of my mom and dad. They seemed to be happy. The first thing said by mom was, "How was your birthday?" They turned and looked at my palms curiously but then, there glee darkened into frowns. They whispered in Grandpa's ear, "Our future does not look good." All four of us popped into the car and drove into the huge castle. My eyes kept lingering on the beauty of the castle. Our dad led us into the castle. We lived in the castle happily for the next ten years, and then we meet Romennakl again. I fought with the powers I had learned and used the sources around me to help. It was a close match, I was in a desperate situation, with Romennakl's sword hovering over my face, but suddenly I stood up and took my sword, and made Romennakl pass out. And we lived happily ever after....

~

Snomeo and Snuliet

A rhyming story based on The Sneetches *by Dr. Seuss*

Rachel T.

You may remember a time in Sneetchland when all the sneetches
that had belly stars,
Treated the sneetches badly that had none upon thars.
Star-belly mothers told their star-belly kids:
"Don't include plain-bellies!" and they never did.
That was okay, though, because the kids hardly ever disagreed,
Even though all the sneetches were all the same breed.
Now, let me tell a story, if you will, if you please,
About a forbidden romance that started with a sneeze.
There once was a plain-belly teen boy, named Snomeo,
Who was wandering around the beaches, because he didn't know
where to go.
There was also a star-belly teen girl on that beach named Snuliet,
Who thought that why plain-bellies were worse, she really didn't get.

Now, Snomeo had a cold, because he had seasonal allergies
And all of a sudden, he had a great sneeze.
"Ahhhhhh chooo!" he sneezed, and Snuliet whipped around,
To find the greatest friend that she ever could have found.
It was love at first sight, so she chose to disobey
Everything that her parents would ever say.
"Hi, I'm Snuliet," she said, rather shy.
"Nice to meet you, I'm Snomeo," he said, straightening his tie.
They looked at each other, and with great understanding,
They held hands, and walked on the beach, without even planning.
When Snuliet got home, her mom was furious to say,
"Young lady, I declare you grounded, for three days!"
Of course she snuck out, because otherwise she would miss
Long walks on the beach, and her very first kiss!
When she decided it was time for Snomeo and her parents to meet,
They both took long, deep breaths as they walked down her street.
When her father opened the door, not to Snuliet's surprise,
He said, "You are grounded again, for you have told us many lies!"
The couple pleaded and pleaded for them to be allowed to be together,
And although her parents said no, they vowed to stay true, in all kinds of weather.
So, every season, every day, on that very beach,
They would come for each other, and share some food, usually a peach.
Until one day, her parents found out,
So, she was locked in her room, right away, without a doubt!
She cried, and she cried, for it was weeks without her date,
Until one day she was let out, to celebrate!

All sneetches were the same now, plain-bellies weren't socially buried,
Which also meant that Snomeo and Snuliet could get married!
So, they did, and had seventeen kids, who were all told:
"It doesn't matter who you play with, if they're shy, or if they're bold,
Or if they have belly stars, or none, or even stars on their chest!"
And I think you very well can guess the rest.
If you guessed happily ever after lived Snomeo, Snuliet, and their kids,
Then you guessed very well, indeed you did!
Now that is the end of my romance story,
I hope you enjoyed it, and felt the triumph, and the glory.

~

Dr. Smarty Feathers

Ram P.

Once upon a time there was a Robin. He loved the water. Every morning, evening and night he would go to the river to get some water. He knew that water was good for you, so even when he did not want to go to the river, he would force himself to drink the rare fresh water. It was his regular drink; he would not drink or eat anything else!

He also loved to sing. Singing was his favorite. He sang the best, of all the birds near him! Once he starts singing he would never stop! His singing was perfect, it was fabulous, it was legendary, rare singing! It was the best of the best! He won the Nobel Singing Prize!

The Robin also was very knowledgeable. He got all A++++'s in every subject including math, science, social studies, reading, spelling, P.E. and of course art. Everybody called him Dr. Smarty Feathers. Now, that was amazing!

Well.....one day some bad people came with a robot and were stealing the water. The robot was the worst of the worst, gigantic, fierce, and the meanest thing that ever existed. He was the opposite of the Robin. He was sucking away all the water from the river. All the birds were pleading not to take away all the water, since their lives depended on the water.

Dr. Smarty Feathers comes to their rescue, since the Robin knew he had to save his people, and the water. He looks for the self-destruct button for the Robot. It was not there. Dr. Smarty Feather uses his smartness and sings an emotional song. The song was so good, the Robot and the bad people get hypnotized and they change into good people. They return all the water. And everybody lives happily ever after.

~

Nature

Richard Y.

WATER

Water splashes over my hand
Water at beaches with shells and sand
Water is pure, light and clear
In the form of the sea or a tear
Water, a natural element
Water, a true replenishment
Water, a liquid, solid, gas
Water in a clear drinking glass

TREES

A plant with leaves
listen as it sighs
listen as it heaves
a tree, the home to a honey bee
growing ,slowly
in all shapes and sizes
a tree

AIR

What we take in when we take a breath
Without it we would face a painful death
Invisible oxygen and other gas
But with pollution air will fade and pass
air as the wind blowing a leaf through the sky
air as far as the atmosphere, it goes up really high

~

The Wild Safari

Rishi J.

My friend Andrew and I had just arrived in Kilimanjaro, Africa. Andrew was tall, pudgy and the risk taker, while I was a thinker, tall and skinny.

As we approached our taxi to embark on our safari with the world famous Kilimanjaro Adventures, we talked about getting lost in the treacherous and scary wilderness, but who knew we would experience our fears in reality.

Our taxi reached the game park reserve one hour later and the weather was terribly hot. Along the road, the green grass was crunched up and dried.

We jumped out of the taxi and into the safari truck to begin our memorable adventure. It was amazing to see the gigantic and fast Wildebeest dash through the fields of long and fresh grass. I was so engrossed in the wildlife that I felt like I jumping off the truck!

We stopped at a relaxing resting area a little while later. I sat down taking a deep breath, when I saw a dark and small figure reaching for a juicy and ripe mango. Then I noticed the distinguishing features, dark short hair, black face and eyes, crouched walking position. The tiny figure was a baby gorilla!

Suddenly I had a strong, vital urge to follow the gorilla on a journey. I listened to my instincts and dashed behind the sly and timid creature. Andrew followed. We dodged damp vines and curved through the long forest paths.

After a while I was exhausted. Thinking I was talking to Andrew, I said: "Do you know where in the world we are?" Since I didn't hear any response, I turned around and saw he wasn't there! I was completely shocked! I stumbled around the forest frantically. Then I noticed that Andrew and I had strayed out of the game park reserve. How could the day get any worse? Too frustrated to think clearly, I continued looking in panic.

I heard a familiar voice, then a howl. The next thing I knew, Andrew was running back laughing so hard it seemed his voice box would come out!

As soon as I saw Andrew, I told him the bad news. Unfortunately, I guess I shouldn't have told him because the next few minutes I had to calm him down. He screamed and wiggled around and around. I told him in an agitated voice, "Don't freak out or I will go psycho too!"

As the next few hours flew past like the world spinning a hundred times faster, we attempted tracking back using our footsteps. But there were footprints on tops of ours? Confused, I asked Andrew if he knew which animals' footsteps they were, but as usual he hadn't noticed a thing.

I realized then there was an animal tracking us down. I heard deep breathing, hustling and snuffling. I stood as still as a solid rock statue as something crept closer. Andrew and I were as quiet as a fox on a hunt. Then out of the blue pounced a neon ambush of orange tigers. "AHH!" Andrew and I screamed.

The ferocious ambush of tigers smelled of rotting flesh. The terrible roar sounded teeth-rattling. The bloody teeth startled me into thinking the tigers would have an easy time catching us for a hearty meal.

Backing away in fear, Andrew suddenly had an idea. Too scared to evaluate Andrew's idea, I agreed. Andrew and I planned to make a small but dangerous fire to scare the ambush of tigers away.

We rapidly grabbed two rocks and started rubbing them together. Once a spark or two flew off, Andrew put the rock with the beginning sparks on a thick stick. Flash, it burned quickly into a fire which Andrew laid into a pile of brush in the middle of the path. Sure enough, the tigers backed away in no time. I ran and grabbed Andrew as we dashed away from the tigers.

A few peaceful hours later, we somehow tracked back to the game park reserve! I instantly ran to my parents beaming with joy. I whispered to them, "Curiosity killed the cat, but didn't kill me."

The End

The Two Brothers

Rithvik V.

"Hey, I want to have that toy" said Sam. "Well, too bad, it is mine," said Jack. "Argh," said their mom.

Once upon a time, there lived two brothers. One was named Sam. The other was named Jack. Jack was three years old. Sam was ten years old. They had only one problem between them. It was that they would never share their toys, neither a birthday present nor a holiday gift. Jack would usually start the problem. When the problem starts to get really bad, they would start hitting each other. Their mom would get really upset when they started fighting. Christmas was coming up. On the day before Christmas, mom told Jack and Sam that she would buy only one toy because she wanted to see how well her kids would share. Jack did not like this idea. So, Jack woke up really early in the morning of Christmas and took the toy and hid it in his room where Sam would never find it.

Sam woke up in the morning at his usual time. He went downstairs to look for the present but he did not see it. He told his parents that he didn't see the present. His parent's told him that they would go shopping for a present after breakfast. They finished breakfast and went to Target in their car. They got a T.V. and installed it in Sam's room.

Jack wanted a T.V. too. His parent's said that he would need to give the Christmas present that he took away to Sam. When the family went home, Jack gave the toy to Sam. Sam's parents told him that he doesn't have to give any of his toys to Jack. But Sam did not like that idea. It didn't feel fair to him. So, when his parents were asleep, he took the Christmas present that Jack took away and put it in front of his bed. The next morning, Jack got out of his bed and tripped over the toy. he went to look back at what he tripped over. Jack saw the toy that he once stole. On the toy it said," Merry Christmas! From, Sam." Jack called Sam into his room and gave him a big hug! After that day, they always shared their toys and be nice to each other.

The Amazing Travels of Ben's Bubble Gum

Ryan G.

Everyone loves the taste of bubble gum. Actually, not everyone. Ben and his family won't go near it. Here's why:

In 1931, bubble gum had just been invented. In fact there were only two pieces of bubble gum in the world. One day, a boy named Ben and his cousin Sam found a piece of gum in the whole wide world!! They were so excited. Ben and Sam played a game of basketball to see who would get to eat the gum. Ben made an unbelievable trick shot over his head to win. So he ate the gum. He said it was the best thing he tasted in his life.

That day Ben took a walk and when he sat down at a picnic bench the gum fell out of his mouth. He didn't want it to look like he littered so he stuck it to the bottom of the picnic bench. He still felt guilty, but he went home anyway. That night Ben went home watched TV, and went to bed. Then all of a sudden he felt like the gum gave him a curse.

Later, there was a storm that was so windy it blew the gum blew off the picnic bench. The next day Ben's brother Charlie took a walk and stepped on the gum. When he got home Ben noticed the gum stuck to the bottom of Charlie's shoe. He thought about the gum and its curse. Then he tried to stop thinking about it. He did.

When Charlie and his dad went to the store they both noticed the gum, and Charlie scraped it off his shoe. Two days later Ben went back to the store and again stepped on the gum. Now he was sure the gum was cursed. When Ben got home his dad was very grumpy and he was so sick of seeing the gum he traveled to India and left it there.

That day their cousin, Ani from India found the gum, and she was visiting them. So since there were only two pieces of gum in the world she wrapped it up to bring to her cousins. So she brought it. Even though it was already chewed, YUCK!!

This time when Ben's dad saw the gum he decided to take the family on a trip to Australia and throw the gum in the ocean. When Ben's family got back they went to the beach and found the same gum floating in the water! So they went back to Australia and threw it in the ocean again. The same thing happened two times and on the third time when they got back the gum was laying on the beach. Ben walked up to the gum. Then just when he was about to pick it up a three- year old boy jumped in front of him and ate the gum. "YUCK". Ben said. Charlie's dad was so happy he did a crazy dance and screamed as loud as he could, "Yes!"

From then on no one in Ben's family ever ate or looked at a piece of gum. Ben disagreed with that rule. But since he loved his family so much he followed their rule.

THE END

A trip to the space station

Sam H.

Living on earth just isn't enough for me. Living on earth is just too boring. Don't you ever feel that way? I think that there are much better places. Jupiter, mars, the moon–don't those seem better? Maybe you can live on earth, with all your water and plants, but I've had enough. I'm sick of it. So I've decided to go on a trip far away from here, to the space station!

Arriving at the launching area, I thought about what I was getting into. I remember my situation just yesterday. I had begged and begged and begged my mom, and finally she agreed to pay the $89099.99 to let me go on one of apple®'s newly released space trips. In case you aren't up to date with it, apple® recently sent and assembled all the parts for a 1500 square foot space station home with monitoring space police into the outer exosphere. They then furnished the home and sent up food. They tested this prototype before sending up 500 more homes, all with guards to help the residents live in space. They now market a space getaway for only $89099.99 a weekend. I knew that I had to get my mom to send me up on the mission, because we recently won Jeopardy, and we had a total of one million dollars in extra money. But back to the point. Saddling up my Space Sky adventure; or SS adventure as the internet spies are calling it, I realized how dangerous what I was doing was. I mean, technically, flying in a space trip is "as safe as living on planet earth," or so the apple® slogan says. But still, I had a feeling that something bad bad would happen... But the feeling was washed away as I was swept into the machine. The machine recognized me, and I held my iPhone six up to it to take my credit card information. It then leapt into the air, and started towards space.

I'd like to explain to you now, firsthand, that it is very hard to sleep in a Ss adventure, what with all the noise and lights. Inside, there was an iPad built into the area in front of me. I was able to download apps and communicate with customer service who would help me in dire emergencies. Hoping that there wouldn't be any, I saw a rock ahead of me. A huge, space debris rock. Aren't those great? So I pulled up customer service and waited. The space car stopped midair and stayed in one spot.

"Your call has been forwarded to our automatic systematic problematic solver for galactic space problems. If you would like to report a dire emergency, say 'Help me! I'm dying!' No, I'm just joking. I'm a customer service dude. What can I help ya with, bro?"

"Please, help me now... There's a huge rock in front of me, and I don't know where to go. I've been stopped in midair, and the ship's not moving. Is there anything you can do?" I said urgently, hoping that this lackadaisical customer service man would become more serious at the thought of a customer suspended in space.

"Yeah sure, bro.. I'll check it out. Here, have some coffee while I do the computer stuff, alright, bro?" he muttered nonchalantly. A tray came out in front of me, and there was a cup of coffee on it, waiting nice and steamy.

"Really? Coffee? I'm 13 years old. I don't even like coffee. I mean, the most adult drink that I ever consume is probably grape juice... why in the world would I want coffee? If you insist on giving me a drink, at least give me something that won't cause potential health problems! At least just give me a little water!" I couldn't help myself from being mad at such an ignorant person.

"Dude, chill, chill, seriously... why so mad? Just chillax, dude. You'll be fine. I'm sending out our space police, and they'll be there in a minute to burn up the rock. Seriously dude, just like, chill out!" he said, like water pouring from a faucet. In that minute, I seriously considered punching a hole in the wall of the spaceship and being sucked into my own skin. What good would that do me? It would get me away from that loser that I was talking with.

Looking out the front window, I noticed a few other spaceships, they seemed more official than mine. I also noticed the lights on the top of their roofs. Were they police? Most possibly. I waved to one, and he waved back.

They then all pressed buttons on their iPads, and large lenses came out from their spaceships. They all focused the energy of the sun on the rock, and, suddenly, *BAM!* The rock exploded! I saw tiny bits and fragments of the rock fall into the empty space. They were flying all over the place! One hit the glass of my spaceship. My SS adventure started to become adventurous! The piece fell onto the glass, and the glass curved in like plastic wrap, then continued to fling the piece out back into space. It was amazing, as if my glass was made of latex! It felt like I was living in a balloon! I reached out and touched the film. It stretched to shape my hand, and suddenly, my hand flew right at my face! What an amazing glass! I decided I'd test how amazing it really was. I pulled out my pencil from my pocket, and I poked the balloon like texture. I knew that I was risking my life, but if I was going to die, I wanted to die in the name of science. I reached out, held my breath, closed my eyes, and poked the film. There was a very loud pop, and I screamed.

"Dude, don't scream, that's just my computer. Don't you know? When you get an email on a mac it makes a *POP* noise? I just had the volume up all the way. I think you need to seriously chillax... Here, have some tea." He replied to my scream very aloofly.

Recovering, I pulled the cup of tea to my mouth and drank. It was very strange. It wasn't really a cup of tea. It was more like a baby bottle. There was one opening at the top and you had to read the instructions on the side before you drank it. They read:

1. Put in mouth.
2. Press button on bottom.
3. Hold switch on side.
4. Tilt head back and enjoy.

The tea wasn't very hot, but it did manage to cool off my senses. I felt kind of like I had just drank some sort of magic medicine. Maybe he had put something in my tea, because next thing I know, I had fallen asleep. Just like that.

I woke up and felt gravity. I noticed a large, stubble bearded possibly twenty year old sitting in a chair in front of me. I guess that he had put my magnet belt on me. And found my weight out, to know which colored belt to use. It was all in the manual. What a nice fellow.

"You're up! How was your ride?" said the man. It was the customer service guy.

"Hey, it's you! You were the one that was talking to me! Why are you here?" I said skeptically.

He smiled and said, "It's OK, bud. I live here. I also help with the space ships and help them reach planet awesome. That's what I call this place, planet awesome. Cool, right?"

"Yeah, I guess. It is pretty cool. Hey, how about you tell me something cool I can do here. I paid lots of money to get here, and I want it to be fun!" I said that last word kind of like a TV salesman for a kids toy.

"Well, look around you. Look outside. Heck, take off your gravity belt and float around! This place never gets old! I don't ever want to go back to earth! It really stinks that you have to. This place is awesome! LET'S HAVE FUN!" He bellowed with a smile that made me think that he genuinely cared about me. You know what, maybe he did.

"Hey, I didn't catch your name, dude. What is it? Mine's Sam." I said.

"Jacob. But all my best friends call me Jake, and you're like, my best friend, so, call me Jake!"

The next day and a half were the best. I had a great time playing on my iPad and Jake's prototype for the iPad 5, having floating water drinking contests, and playing pin the Adam's Apple on Tim Cook. Jake always brings a picture of him whenever he hears a child is coming to his station.

When the time came to go home to earth, I didn't want to leave. I wanted to stay and have fun with Jake but, unfortunately, I had to leave. I said goodbye to Jake, opened the door to the travel compartment, and jumped into my spaceship. I then took off for home.

When I got there, I got out, and said goodbye to Jake once more through customer service. I was lucky I could get his email.

I was even more lucky that I didn't have crushed ribs after the huge hug my mom gave me. I told her I loved her, got into the car, and went off to home to email Jake. And THAT was how I went to space.

~

Pandora's Box

Sayalee P.

Once upon a time there lived a girl whose name was Jewel. The next day she was turning ten. Finally, it was the next day and all her relatives were there. Everyone gave her their gifts except her grandfather. He was hiding his present behind his back.

"Grandpa, it is your turn to give me your gift," said Jewel.

"I know, but I wanted to give it to you privately," said Grandpa.

"Ok," said Jewel walking with Grandpa to another room.

"This is Pandora's Box," said Grandpa giving her the box, "never open this box, I wanted to give it to you in private because the others might be jealous." "This is a box of your great, great, great, great grandfather," he continued, "it has been passed on for many generations and I picked you to be the next one to have it."

"Ok," said Jewel trying not to look like she wanted to open it, "but why can't I open it?"

"I was told never to open it so I tell you the same," said Grandpa.

"Ok," said Jewel.

They went back to be with everyone. They had cake, corn, and other stuff too. But the whole time Jewel was thinking about the box. Finally, the party was over. Jewel took the box and went to her room.

"I really want to know what's in here," she said.

She shook the box. She heard nothing. She thought about what could be in there.

"Grandpa said NOT to open it," said Jewel, "but I really want to know what's in here."

Finally, she said, "I am going to open it."

She took the key and slowly opened the box.

"WHOA!!" she screamed.

Soon she found herself in a house and right in front of her was a random person.

“Who are you?” she asked.

“I am your great, great, great, great grandfather,” said the man, “I made this box and opened it. Right now you are in the box.”

“WHAT?” said Jewel, “how do you get out?”

“If I knew I wouldn’t be in here,” said the man.

Jewel was panting.

“I will go get you some water,” said the man.

He came back with water. Jewel set the key down and took the cup.

“So how did you end up here?” asked the man.

“Two things,” said Jewel, “first can I call you grandfather?”

“Sure,” said grandfather, “why not?”

“And second, I opened the box and found myself here.”

“Interesting,” said grandfather.

“What’s so interesting about that?” questioned Jewel.

“I have a long story behind how I got here,” said grandfather.

“Why don’t you tell me?” said Jewel.

“Ok,” said grandfather. “It all started when I made this box.”

“I just finished making the keyhole and was testing it to see if it worked,” he continued, “I left the box on my table. It seems my friend who isn’t my friend anymore put a magic spell on the box so anyone who opened the box got in,” he said. “Soon after I vanished, my mom found the box and realized that when I opened the box I vanished. So then my mom told my wife that I disappeared when I opened the box. My wife decided to open the box and be with me. And that is how my wife and I are trapped in here. We have been in here for one hundred and twenty years trying to figure out how to get out.”

“And I also know someone who might want to meet you,” he said.

“Who?” asked Jewel.

“Come with me,” said grandfather.

Grandfather and Jewel walked across the street and rang the doorbell. A nice woman opened the door.

“Why hello,” the woman said, “what brings you here?”

“I am here to have you meet Jewel,” grandfather said, “she was next in line to have the box until she got stuck in it.”

"Jewel," he continued, "this is your great, great, great, great grandmother.

"Hello," Jewel said shaking the woman's hand, "it is nice to meet you."

"It is nice to meet you too," she said.

"How can we get out?" asked Jewel, "oh yeah and can I call you grandmother?"

"Sure," said grandmother, "and how do we get out, well we are going to have to get the key."

"Oh, I have the key," said Jewel patting and checking het pockets. "Uh oh," she said kind of scared, "I don't have it anymore. But maybe it's still in your house," she said.

"No, everything in my house has to be in a drawer, cabinet, or closet and everything else vanishes," said grandfather, "so please don't tell me you put it on the table because that is the reason why my house is so organized."

"I put it on the table," said Jewel in the panic.

"Wait," said grandfather, "maybe I could make a new key."

"Why didn't you think of that before?" asked Jewel.

"Because we need the power of three or more family members to make the key," said grandfather.

"Great," said Jewel, "so what do we do first?"

"Well, here comes the bad part. I will need the family generation crystal," said grandfather.

"What's that?" asked Jewel.

"It is a crystal found by our ancestors," said grandmother, "it is going to give us hope and luck."

"So where is it?" asked Jewel.

"It is located in Mount Everest," said grandfather, "but still in the box."

"Don't you mean on Mount Everest," said Jewel.

"No, I mean in," said grandfather, "there is a secret passageway that only grandmother and I know and soon you will too," continued grandfather.

Jewel was excited to start the adventure.

"So where do we start?" asked Jewel.

"I keep this map in case I ever need it," said grandmother taking out the map.

"Ok," said Jewel, "we will have to take a train to the coastline of the ocean and there we will sail across to Europe."

"Let's go," said grandmother.

They took the train and got half way there until the train got stuck!

"Oh no," said Jewel, "what do we do now? We need to get out of this box before someone realizes that I opened it," she said. "We'll never reach on time."

"Calm down we will reach," said grandmother.

Finally, the driver said, "we will be boarding another train."

Jewel calmed down. Soon they reached and it was morning about 9:00 AM.

"We can rest here for a few hours then we will sail the sea," said grandfather.

"Ok," said Jewel.

"How about we eat breakfast?" said grandmother.

They ate breakfast and were off on the ocean.

"This is beautiful," said Jewel. "Look at the dolphins jump up and down."

"Whoa," Jewel screamed.

Their boat was sinking! Everyone fell into the water with a splash. They plopped their heads above the water so they could speak.

"Look, there's a nearby island," said Jewel. "Let's go."

They swam to the island and were safe on land

"That was scary," said Jewel.

"Well how long do we have to stay here?" asked grandmother.

"Maybe a day," said grandfather.

It was night by the time they settled down and had dinner. Soon they slept and awoke at 7:00 AM by an odd smell.

"Do you smell that?" asked Jewel.

"Yes, yes I do," said grandmother.

Grandfather and grandmother looked around while Jewel sat there describing the smell.

"It smells like smoke or coconut," said Jewel.

"Look, fire," screamed grandfather as he started throwing water at a little spark. They all started throwing water and finally the fire went out.

"Why is all this happening to us?" asked Jewel, "all these bad things."

"How would I know," said grandfather.

"This is weird," said grandmother.

They all ate breakfast talking about what happened.

"Hey look there is a raft," said grandfather, "maybe we can get a ride."

"Good," said grandmother.

"Hey, over there," shouted grandfather.

The man saw them and was heading for them.

"Will you give us a ride?" grandfather asked the man.

"Sure," said the man with a weird smile, "of course I will."

"Ok," said grandfather kind of nervous.

Soon they reached the land.

"Are you sure we reached the right place, because this place looks creepy," said Jewel scared.

"Let me check," said grandfather looking at the map.

"Oh no," said grandfather, "we are way to the north from where we are supposed to be."

"Look, there's a train station," said grandmother, "we can take a train south to go where we want."

"Good idea," said grandfather, "let's go."

They went on the train and finally the train ride was smooth. Soon they were back on track.

"Ok," said grandfather, "now we take a bus to Asia because we are on the border of Europe."

"Yay," said Jewel, "we are almost there."

They went on the bus, but the person sitting across from them kept staring at them.

"Why does that person keep staring at us?" asked Jewel, "and he looks like that person we saw when we looked out the window when the train got stuck, and like the guy who gave us a boat ride to the wrong place."

"You are right Jewel," said grandfather, "maybe he caused all the bad stuff to happen."

"If he did cause all that to happen," said grandmother, "maybe we should try staying away from him."

Soon the bus ride was over and they were on the border of the Himalayas. They went to Mount Everest and soon were at the bottom. Grandfather picked up a stick and wrote PANDORA'S BOX. A door opened and they went inside. There was a long tunnel.

"How long is this tunnel?" asked Jewel.

"It's almost over," answered grandfather.

Just then they heard a voice. "Stop," said the voice. Soon they were able to see him clearly.

"That's the guy on the bus," Jewel whispered.

"Don't worry," said grandfather, "I'll take it from here."

Grandfather took a torch and started waving it at the man. Grandfather set the man's jacket on fire and finally the man left. They got the crystal and were heading home until the man came again when they had just crossed the sea. But this time he was with a gun.

Boom! Boom! Boom!

"Come on," said the man, "are you afraid of me?"

Grandfather went up and kicked him, punched him, and hit him. Jewel was staring at grandfather.

"Wow," said Jewel surprised, "how did you do that?"

"I was trained to fight when I got in this box," said grandfather.

"Did you know that?" Jewel asked grandmother.

"No," said grandmother, "no, I did not."

Finally they reached home and grandfather made the key using the power of the three of them and the crystal.

"Done," said grandfather, "let's go."

They went to grandfather's house, went up the attic, and went to the keyhole. Grandfather put the key in the keyhole and slowly turned the key. The door opened.

"Yay," said Jewel.

They all walked out.

"Finally," said grandmother.

"We are out," said grandfather.

Nobody noticed that Jewel opened the box and came back since time ran way faster inside the box. Grandfather and grandmother returned to their one hundred and twenty year old house. And they all lived happily ever after.

~

Stuck

Tanvee P.

It was the last period of the day and the principal interrupted class to make a new bulletin. “Due to the colossal amount of snow students will stay in school after the bell rings, however students will be allowed to use their cell phones and iPods. They will be allowed to mingle with friends and use the computers, iPads, and iPods in the school. Thank you,” The room was in an uproar. Actually the whole school was in an uproar. You could hear all the students shouting in protest.

For the rest of science our teachers let us talk with friends in class. Every conversation had the same punch line. If there was snow then you were let out early, not kept late. I pulled my best friend Stefani to the side. We sat in a corner and talked. “What are we going to do?” I asked. “We can’t stay here forever!” “Destiny,” she replied, “nothing is going to happen. The school is probably just finding a way to get so many kids home. I mean look at all of that snow!” She was right. It was snowing like crazy and it didn’t look like it was going to end anytime soon.

When the bell rang there was a stampede of people running for the door. Cell phones were yanked from lockers and backpacks. You could hear everyone calling his or her parents. We stopped at Stefani’s locker to get all the stuff she needed, then we went to get my stuff. Just as I was about to call my friend Audrey, she ran over. “Hey. I’m going to hang out with some other friends. Ok? Bye!” “Ok then. That answers my question,” I said a little awkwardly. “Come on! Lets grab a computer!” Stefani says to fill the awkwardness. “OK” I replied.

We were surfing the Internet for about half an hour when we a heard an unbearably emphatic whistle. “ATTENTION!” someone shouted over the loud speaker. “DUE TO THE SNOW, STUDENTS AND STAFF

ARE GOING TO STAY HERE OVERNIGHT. EACH CHILD IS RESPONSIBLE FOR HIS OR HER SELF DUE TO THE FACT THAT EACH STUDENT IN THIS SCHOOL IS IN 5TH OR 6TH GRADE. IF ANYONE NEEDS ASSISTANCE PLEASE CONTACT THE OFFICE."

"What!" I shouted. I wasn't the only one. Everyone was shouting in protest. "We can't stay here overnight!" I told Stefani. "Well, doesn't look like we have a choice," she replied. "Yeah you're right," I said. Then I realized something. If we had to stay here overnight, then we had to find a place to sleep. "Stefani, log off the computer now!" I whispered. I didn't want anyone to know about my idea otherwise there was going to be a crazy stampede for what I wanted. "Why?" she asked. "Just do it," I muttered. "OK, gosh," she said a little agitatedly. "Come on and stay close," I said.

I started to run toward the gym, Stefani doing the best she could to stay close. We ran up to the gym teacher and breathlessly I asked, "Can we have two gym mats?" "Sure," he said a little uncertainly, not sure exactly why we wanted them but willing to give them to us. By now Stefani knew where I was going with the whole thing. While Mr. Jones went to go get the mats, Stefani turned to me and said, "Wow, quick thinking. It's a really good idea, sleeping on gym mats." "Thanks," I replied. "Now all we have to do is carry them up the stairs so that nobody catches on and tries to grab them from us. I mean there are only so many mats and a ton of people."

After we lugged the mats up the stairs we found the emptiest classroom and set the mats up there. Once we were set up we took turns going to the bathroom, and going to our lockers to get scarves, our backpack, food, jackets, or anything else that might come in handy. Now that we had stuff other people would want one person was stuck at in the classroom with our stuff. We decided that Stefani would go and find out about what we were going to eat for dinner. If she wasn't back in 15 minutes then I would call her and see what was going on. Stefani left. She was gone for about five minutes when I thought I heard someone calling my name. It was so faint that I was pretty sure I was imagining it.

A couple minutes later I was sure I wasn't imagining the sound because it was way louder. "Destiny! Destiny! Destiny, where are you?" I knew someone was calling me but I couldn't leave my spot so I waited. Then Audrey stepped in the room and asked some 5th grader, "Have you guys seen a 6th grade girl with green eyes, brown hair with gold highlights and a retainer?" "You mean her?" the 5th grader asked, pointing at me. "Yeah, thanks," she replied.

"Hey," Audrey said. "Oh hey," I replied. "Sorry I couldn't hang out with you," she said apologetically. "That's OK," I replied. "So," Audrey said, "looks like you're ahead of the game. Got a place to sleep and everything." " I guess. Do you have a place to sleep yet?"

"Yes"

"Cool. Where?"

"The sofas in the library."

"Oh."

"They're way softer then gym mats."

"Yeah I know but they are too small the lay down on. I thought about it but decided laying down is better than having to sit and sleep."

"Well I like where I'm sleeping," Audrey said hurtfully. "I have no problem with you sleeping there that's just my point of view," I said slowly. "Well I don't like your point of view," she said scornfully. "Well then you shouldn't have asked for it," I retorted. "Well then!" Audrey snapped. She got up in a huff and stalked off. Just then Stefani came back. "What was that about?" she asked. "Long story," I said warily.

"OK so here's the deal. They are giving out dinner to everyone but I couldn't get yours because 'it could be an excuse for more food'" Stefani said the last part with a high pitched nasally voice. "So you have to go down get in line, and then they will give you food and check your name off a list of all the students in the school. I got mine while I was there because we couldn't go together so it really didn't matter," Stefani held out the plate of pizza. "Oh yeah and it's first come first serve on what dish you want so you better hurry up, the line was pretty long." The way Stefani said it all reminded me of those people who talked so fast they ran out of breath. "OK, I'll leave right now then," I said, standing up. Stefani snorted "You better. If you don't you'll be stuck with grilled cheese." I made a face. Gross. I still hadn't forgotten the time some dude found a moldy piece of bread, part of the grilled cheese sandwich on his plate.

When I got down I realized Stefani was right. The cafeteria was quite full and it was still filling. I quickly stepped in line and found myself right behind Audrey. Audrey turned and saw me. "Sorry about the way I acted. I guess I was a little bit of a jerk," she said a little resentfully. "That's OK," I replied. "We're still friends." For the next ten minutes Audrey and I chatted while we waited in line. When we both finally got the food we talked a couple more minutes then went our separate ways. When we reached our "den" I found a panicked Stefani. She hurried me over. "Um, Destiny, little problem. Some stupid 5th grader saw our stuff loved the idea, and just had to shout about it to the entire school. Now there is a little bit of a rampage for the gym mats." I realized that made a lot of sense. The hallways had seemed quiet and it was pretty loud in the gym. I decided to defend ourselves like this: "Well we didn't do anything wrong. The principal said every kid for themselves and that's what we did."

Basically we held our ground. While I ate Stefani told every kid who asked how we got a gym mat. Actually, how we got 2. So we told them. And told off anyone who got mad and said it was unfair. By the time the whole thing was cooled down it was 9:30 p.m. We decided to go to bed. I slept well considering that I was sleeping in a gym mat. In the morning the crackling of the intercom woke me up. I found out it was 9:00 a.m. So most people were awake or waking up because of the noise. "ATTENTION! THE CITY SNOW DIGGERS HAVE DUG US OUT. PARENTS ARE PULLING UP OUTSIDE TO PICK STUDENTS UP. WE WILL CALL YOU BY CLASSROOM TO GRAB YOUR STUFF AND GO OUTSIDE. DUE TO THE INCOVENIENCE, THERE WILL BE NO HOMEWORK. THANK YOU." Everyone cheered. Well, I thought, that had been quite an experience.

~

The Unnamed Boy

Wilson Z.

A long time ago, reborn from the ashes of Mesopotamia, in the far out land, there was a deer. The deer was no ordinary deer, in was a magical one that could fly. Not only could this deer fly, but it was very strong and wise. It helped people when they needed help the most.

CHAPTER 1

The boy was sitting at the curb. He was wearing light green overalls with a green jacket. Everybody at school thought he was different and weird and a little disturbing. Even his parents thought that about him. Not that he ever did anything wrong or was a bad kid or anything, he just radiated a feeling of unluckiness and hopelessness. This made him lonely, and he had no friends. But the boy didn't mind. Just because he lived in a green house and under a green roof, nobody knew his name. Not even his mom. Because he had no name.

Tossing the ball up into the air with amazing accuracy and quickly using the shadows to hide behind a nearby bush, the boy watched as his worst bully came plummeting around the corner, and the ball struck him square on his forehead. The bully, whose name was Joe, instantly blacked out. Suddenly, the boy could feel an upcoming trap. An armada of soldiers and police men surrounded the boy hiding behind the bush. The boy, who was now in despair, knelt down and whispered for the legendary deer.

"You are under arrest!" said a police man, "For stealing and robbing a hundred diamonds, and the murder of all of the government officials of Iran."

"I did not commit these crimes!" The boy shouted as the crowd carried him away, "This is a wrong accusation!" His words were a hundred percent truthful, and his voice carried far and wide above the crowd of roaring people.

"Send him away" was the last thing he heard before a gust of wind whirled everyone down and the boy was standing in front of the crowd next to a brilliant clear colored deer.

The magical deer was really an awe striking sight. The deer's fur was clear and silvery metallic, embedded with jewels that shone in the bright sunlight. The gray dirty polluted sky was instantly cleared into a deep blue sapphire with the yellow amethyst of a sun blaring down on the people of Ur. The crowd fell silent, and time seemed to slow down itself. The boy clambered onto the deer and was whisked off into the heavens.

CHAPTER 2

In no time, the boy and the deer were over the desert. They saw caravans of people moving along trade routes, and to the boy, he saw some different animals and plants in the desert he had never seen before. The boy saw the great pyramids of Egypt and the Nile river valley which he had only heard about in tales. The two companions came upon a female dragon with bright blue scales and a green head. It seemed as if the dragon needed help. They closed in, and saw that the dragon was stuck to a tremendously large cactus that was almost like a tree. The dragon thanked the deer and boy for helping her pull out the needles. The dragon said her name was Hati and that she was foraging for food because they ran out. She was taking care of a girl, and the dragon's herd had abandoned her for being nice to human beings.

After five miles of walking, the deer began to feel fidgety. Using brain wave signals, she told the boy that they were in danger. The deer suspected they were walking into a trap. The three companions walked into the cave and were immediately confronted with a hoard of giant scorpions. It had turned out that the girl was the queen of the scorpions and that she had summoned her whole kingdom to have a feast on the dragon.

"Ha Ha Ha how nice of you to join us," said the girl, "I hope you don't mind having a feast with us Ha Ha Ha!" Scorpions closed in on either side. Sand flew inward and the cave was filled with sand. The wind changed direction, the sun shone brighter, and the dragon shot a flame of fire into the cave. The scorpions kept coming, and on the bottom of the sand pit the three travelers were trapped into, something rose out. Looking back, a giant scorpion rose out of the sand, and every one froze in fright, even the scorpions.

"What did I tell you, Alice? Do not attack fellow friends!" boomed the scorpion, "And Alice! Don't cover my hole next time either... Sorry about the aggressiveness Lossi"

Alice (the scorpion girl) sheepishly stared down at the floor.

"Who's Lossi?" asked the boy.

"Oh that is the magical deer's first name. She is a regular customer here, it is just that this time we moved our den again...." said the scorpion.

Buzzzzzzzzz. Buzzzzzzzzz . buzzzzzzzzzzz .

A swarm of bees buzzed around the heads of all of the beings in the den, and these bees were the real threat that the magical deer had felt earlier.

The bees formed a circle around the den. It had now become clear that the den that the companions were occupying was actually the bees' nest. The scorpions at the end of the den started crawling outward, and the whole back of the cave collapsed, revealing a Queen bee the size of the whole cave. The Queen was armored from head to stinger with a deadly green colored coat, instead of a yellow and black one. The coat glowed bright green and a sandstorm started, spinning into frenzy. The Queen illuminated the sandstorm, and her warriors charged into the cave, killing any unarmored being standing in its way.

The giant scorpion and his armada of soldiers, after having survived the attacks along with everyone else except Alice, had a funeral for her. After the funeral, the company of people continued traveling west in a band. The boy and his companions were stared at whenever a caravan passed them, or they passed a caravan. After a few days, the company ran out of water.

Lossi and Hati both went out to scout for water. They returned after thirty minutes, after finding a large lake. They said after testing the water, that it was the freshest fresh water that they had ever seen. The lake was a few miles deep, but you could see the bottom!

An hour later, the companions finally reached the lake at last. They drank deeply to quench their thirst. They looked all the way to the bottom of the lake, but in the middle of the lake, the companions saw a gargantuan hole. After asking the locals of the town, they received the information that the hole lead all the way through the Earth and arose somewhere around a large lake on the other side of the world. If you knew the passageways, you could get to any area on Earth.

The boy decided to use the passageways, "We shall go around the world, and save it from every beast!" he declared.

"Now all of you listen up." said the captain of the ship that they were going in. "There is a giant monster at the bottom of the lake. This monster is a ferocious fighter. It has caused earthquakes and tsunamis in the past. Once it even started a volcanic eruption, which destroyed the earth and created the Mediterranean Sea. We had better be careful, because he guards the causeways and we have to fight him."

The ship was boarded with weapons, and missile launchers, and even two bombs the size of two feet as a radius. One bomb was for blowing up the monster, and if all else failed and they were inside the monster, the other bomb was for self-destruct.

CHAPTER 3

The submarine shot downward, and slowed down. They passed down and in the side tunnels. There was no sign of the behemoth. A few moments later, two Leviathan creatures poked their heads out of one portal. They circled the ship and closed in. As one of them was about to eat the ship, a missile was launched out, and the monster ate the missile, causing itself to explode. Suddenly, a bigger goliath than the last monster expanded itself until it block the way from behind the ship, and swallowed the second monster whole. It unexpanded, and the ship was blasted into a portal.

The captain swore, "This portal is the portal in which we go into other portals and finally end in the Bermuda Triangle! That is the place where no one ever returns!" The vast sea was empty, and not a sound could be heard. A large rumble broke the silence, and a gigantic wave of air blasted from under the water. I knocked the ship aside, and refilled all of the air tanks. Air blasted from all sides, and the ship soared out of the water. "Hang on!" shouted the captain. He pressed a button, and they soared in the air, over the waves. The boy told the captain to go west, and they soared over the land to the United States, at least what that country was at that time.

Imprinted using corn to make designs, the giant letters T.A.N.M.A.B. was printed all over the land. The crew soared down into the land, ready to fight, just in case they were going to be attacked by the armada of humans below, which were armed from head to toe with strange weapons and were standing in the empty space of the letters.

"T-A-N-M-A-B! There are no magical animals or beings!
T-A-N-M-A-B! There are no magical animals or beings!
T-A-N-M-A-B! There are no magical animals or beings!
T-A-N-M-A-B! There are no magical animals or beings!
T-A-N-M-A-B! There are no magical animals or beings!
T-A-N-M-A-B! There are no magical animals or beings!"

The shouts could be heard from the ground. "Pull up!" said the boy, "They are our enemies!"

The companions flew off north, to find a hiding area to hide from TANMAB and prepare for war.

They landed in a large den, and found hoards of bees, dragons, lizards, reptiles, monsters, and talking sheep that were in RATANMAB, which was Resistance against TANMAB and were also preparing for war against TANMAB. They allowed the company to join, and they all prepared for their war that was going to start tomorrow.

TO BE CONTINUED...

The Burning of My Soul

Yoanna I. and Archana V.

My heart gets devoured by the agonizing monster.
Each broken piece bound together by dark, smoky flames,
The flames lick and burn my soul.
Sizzle, crackle, pop!
It burns me until it is too much to bear and all turns black.

The fire claws at my soul,
crawling around inside of me.
It pushes the boundaries trying to make me fight,
trying to escape me,
And unleash to burn the monster who cursed me,
and forced me to feel like this.

It tries to escape;
it is hard to contain.
The intense heat,
the fierce anger,
the need to hate.

What to do,
what to hold back.
My thoughts are all jumbled up,
Like a broken puzzle, that can't be put back together.

Nothing is clear through the dark, cloudy smoke.
It is so thick I can taste the smoggy, burnt bitterness.
The flavor is rancid, revolting, and unbearable.

There was a desire from the ashes of my soul,
to make it go away, to make it stop.
I screamed, and it was the only thing I could hear.

Yet there is nothing to make the raging fire go away,
not even a drop of cool, crystal clear water.

Everything is a hazy blur
including myself.
Nothing seems right:
I don't know what happened to my happy moments,
my old life, the old times, and all those comforting, happy feelings.

The only thing you can smell is smoke
from the vicious inferno, which is demolishing my very soul,
the smell is nauseating and utterly disgusting.
The smoke blocks my throat, making breathing a difficult task.
I claw at my neck and finally can breathe again,
leaving a scar, a scar marking what has happened.

Flames engulf me;
they strangle me.
I feel dead but I know I am still alive;
the flames bite at my skin;
an indescribable pain.

Flames continue to devour my soul, changing me.
They burn up who I am.
They transform me into a monster;
one as hideous as the monster who made me transform.

I am no longer myself,
the flames continue to burn and hurt me,
like a predator attacking its prey.
I can no longer feel my skin or bones.
I feel empty, hollow, and void.
I know there is nothing pure inside me anymore:
not even my soul.

There is only one sound that can be heard:
low guttural growls.

They are coming from my lips:
a sign of war and hatred;
a sign of an attack.

I see red and nothing else.
Red, the Devil's color.
Red, the color of anger,
of hatred.

I am morphing into a murderous, marauding, maniacal monster.
I am not myself anymore;
the old me has gone and there is no hope for it.
I am no longer a person with innocence;
I am a monster without a shred of compassion.

I can't hold back anymore.
I want to attack;
I want to fight the source:
the one who set my soul ablaze;
the one I hate.

But I must learn to forgive and forget,
to pick myself up from the ashes of my soul,
to be like the majestic phoenix
who gets reborn after it dies,
    trillions of times
    and can start its life once again, leaving its worries and
    problems behind.

~

Archana